Singapore
City of Gardens

Singapore
City of Gardens

by William Warren
Photography by Luca Invernizzi Tettoni

PERIPLUS

Published by Periplus Editions (HK) Ltd
Copyright © 2000 Periplus Editions (HK) Ltd

ISBN 962-593-155-4
Printed in Singapore

Editor: Kim Inglis

Distributed by:
North America
Tuttle Publishing, Distribution Center, Airport
Industrial Park, 364 Innovation Drive, North
Clarendon, VT 05759.
Tel (802) 773 8930 fax (800) 526 2778
Asia Pacific
Berkeley Books Pte Ltd, 5 Little Road #08-01,
Singapore 536983.
Tel (65) 280 3320 fax (65) 280 6290
Japan
Tuttle Publishing, RK Building, 2nd Floor,
2-13-10 Shimo-Meguro, Meguro-Ku, Tokyo 153.
Tel (813) 5437 0171 fax (813) 5437 0755
Indonesia
PT Java Books Indonesia, Jl Kelapa Gading Kirana,
Blok A14 No 17, Jakarta 14240.
Tel (62) 21 451 5351 fax (62) 21 453 4987

Endpaper: A lithograph
after an oil painting by
Percy Carpenter (1856)
depicting extensive views
of the early Settlement.
Image courtesy of
Antiques of the Orient.

Frontispiece: Singapore's
national flower, the orchid
Vanda Miss Joaquim, a
hybrid discovered in 1893.

Previous page: A statue of
the merlion at the mouth of
the Singapore river. Behind
are a row of coconut palms
(*Cocos nucifera*).

→ The Botanic Gardens
are home to a huge variety
of trees and plants. Here
are a group of *Ensete
superbum,* a type of banana
with an underground stem.

The author, photographer and editor would like to thank the following persons for their assistance in the preparation of this book: Dr Tan Wee Kiat, Dr Yam Tim Wing, Jennifer Ng-Lim Cheo Tee, Koh Soon Kiong, Simon John Longman, Quek-Phua Lek Kheng, Haji Mohammad Shah, Teva Raj, Ohn Set, Wong Wei Har, Wong Tuan Wah of the National Parks Board; Julie Yeo and Helen West of Antiques of the Orient; Amy Ede and David Lim of the Mandai Orchid Gardens; Christine Lim; Ivan Polunin; Richard L P Tan; the staff at Grand Hyatt, Raffles and Shangri-La Hotels; Made Wijaya and Fairuz bin Salleh of Pacific-Nature Landscapes; Lim Keow Wah; Hoo Hai Chew; Dr Chou Sip King; Dr Gee Min; Rasidah Kumat and staff at the Civil Aviation Authority of Singapore (CAAS); and a special thanks to Elisabeth Eber for being so generous with her time and expertise.

← The Alkaff Mansion, built between 1910 and 1930 by a wealthy Arab family of spice traders; it has now been restored and transformed into a restaurant. Various palms including *Areca catechu* and *Livistona chinensis* (on left) and the ubiquitous coconut, along with cannas and a species of fir decorate the foreground.

Overleaf: The Padang, Esplanade Park and colonial core of the city, with the gleaming skyscrapers of Singapore's financial district on the other side of the river. Used as a recreational area since colonial times, the Padang brings a welcome swathe of green to the downtown area.

Contents

10	The Garden City
16	Some Historical Notes (by Elisabeth Eber)
28	Colonial Era Houses and House Gardens
32	The Istana Gardens
36	The Padang and Esplanade Park
40	Raffles Hotel
44	Bras Basah Park
46	Fort Canning Park
50	Chijmes
52	Istana Park
54	Suntec City and Millennium Walk
60	City Courtyards
64	Chinatown
66	Orchard Road
72	Emerald Hill
74	The Botanic Gardens
106	Mount Faber Park
108	Sentosa Island
112	Pasir Panjang Nursery
114	Wayside Trees
118	The Chinese Garden
126	Chinese Traditions
128	A Private Penjing Collection
130	A Tray Landscape Collection
132	A Chinese-style Miniature Garden
134	MacRitchie Reservoir and Park
136	The Singapore Zoological Gardens
142	Mandai Orchid Gardens
148	Jurong Bird Park
152	The National Parks
156	Changi Airport and Road

→ An 1846 watercolour by John Turnbull Thomson depicts a view of Singapore from Fort Canning. It celebrates the presentation of a state sword by the then Governor Lt Colonel Butterworth to Daing Ibrahim, Temengggong of Johore, for his efforts to suppress piracy. The ornamental round in the foreground, probably imaginary, has an Agave as a centrepiece, while in the background the godowns of the harbour and the neatly planted colonial core are clearly executed. Image courtesy of Antiques of the Orient.

The Garden City

"'Singapore ahoy!' exclaimed the man at the mast head as the white houses and shipping rose above the horizon while we were abreast of the large red cliffs.... Hundreds of Chinese junks, and Malay prows, lay further in shore. Behind these stretched a sandy beach, glistening in the sun, and overhung by the graceful palm trees, the glory of Singapore planters. In the centre of the landscape was Government Hill, with its verdant lawns and snug bungalow; and at its base were the warehouses and mansions of the merchant princes. Behind these was to be seen the comely undulating background, alternately covered with the mighty forest trees and gambier and pepper gardens."

Such were the views that greeted John Turnbull Thomson, a young Englishman who came to Singapore in 1838, just two decades after the settlement was founded. Today the relatively rare visitor who arrives by sea encounters an almost solid facade of skyscrapers along the shore, many of them built on land reclaimed from the very waters where Thomson sailed. A few palms might still be glimpsed here and there among the buildings, perhaps even the top of Government Hill (now known as Fort Canning), but the mass of wild jungle and cultivated plantations that once covered all but small portions of the island appears to be gone as thoroughly as the rest of that early 19th-century world.

Yet such an impression would be misleading. A resoundingly modern city Singapore certainly is, one of the great success stories of contemporary Asia; but it can also lay claim to another kind of triumph just as significant to its residents. Scattered among those gleaming downtown towers, more impressively on display elsewhere, are the results of a deliberate campaign to transform Singapore into a literal "Garden City", one unequalled by any other great Asian city and by few in the Western world.

Singapore in colonial times liked to think of itself primarily in terms of material achievements, but it was always a tropical city, close to the equator, a place where things grew with startling speed and luxuriance; and aside from the original jungle there were, increasingly, man-made arrangements of nature. In the beginning, these were largely devoted to commercial crops – plantations of rare spices like nutmeg, clove and pepper as well as such useful plants as gutta percha (*Palaquium* spp, particularly *P. gutta*) which yielded a rubberlike latex. None proved very successful for the growers in the end, but the idea of using Singapore as a kind of huge botanical resource was never wholly abandoned. Most famously, it found expression at the Botanic Gardens from which the Brazilian para rubber tree was first introduced to Malayan plantations. But gradually, as Singapore assumed its role as a great entrepot of international trade, gardening became more of a personal pursuit, principally for pleasure.

The ruling British for the most part lived out of the Civic District in large bungalows, with spacious verandahs and surrounding gardens. Given the heat and regular, year-round rains the gardens were always vividly green – keeping them halfway tamed was a major job – but seldom displayed much originality of design. A few more serious gardeners did emerge, however, prompted by new ornamental plants being introduced through the Botanic Gardens and possibly by a growing sense of confidence. Hoo Ah Kay, an immensely rich Chinese businessman better known by his trade name of "Whampoa", (see pages 25–26) who had owned part of the land on which the Botanic Gardens were established in 1859, was noted as a gardener himself. A foreign visitor invited to see his creation in 1869 describes its "straight paths, winding walks, and labyrinths, a wonderful variety of tropical vegetation...a place where the florist or botanist might find...pleasure."

Under the leadership of RE Holttum, director of the Botanic Gardens, the Singapore Gardening Society was formed in 1936 by a group of local enthusiasts. The Society's main concern in its early years was

← The Swiss Club, one of Singapore's many private clubs. Extensive lawns, a selection of palms including *Cocos nucifera*, *Livistona chinensis* by the porte-cochère, and *Ravenala madagascariensis*, grace the grounds.

→ Often photographed in Singapore, even though it is native to Madagascar, the Traveller's Palm (*Ravenala madagascariensis*) is (and was in early times) a popular ornamental tree. It is seen here flanking a replica of a statue of Stamford Raffles situated at his supposed landing site. The original statue is in front of the Victoria Concert Hall. Below is a view of a residence in Tanglin, complete with palms, and at bottom is the graveyard of the Armenian Church of St Gregory the Illuminator. The Armenians were a small, but influential community whose members included Agnes Joaquim, the discoverer of Singapore's national flower (see frontispiece and page 81). She is buried in the graveyard here. Middle photo courtesy of Antiques of the Orient.

→ Nassim Road, one of Singapore's downtown avenues, is lined with venerable Broad-Leaved Mahogany trees (*Swietenia macrophylla*). A native of Honduras, it was introduced into Singapore around 1876 and is a popular shade tree.

↓ Raffles Place, formerly known as Commercial Square, was built on some of the city's first reclaimed land and was given its name in 1858. Today, as before, it is surrounded by the city's financial institutions and banks. Modern sculptures are by Ng Eng Teng.

the organization of annual plant shows, the first of which was held at the Victoria Memorial Hall in 1938. Such events came to an abrupt end during the Japanese occupation – when, according to one past president of the Society, gardens were "put to food-productive use wherever possible" – but were revived with the coming of peace. The Gardening Society continues today, publishing a regular newsletter and holding monthy meetings.

The British also established a few public parks, set aside forest reserves, and initiated the planting of trees, especially fast-growing varieties like Angsanas and Rain trees, along city streets. An 1873 visitor described Orchard Road, then residential, as "very pretty, being lined by tall bamboo hedges and trees which, uniting above, form a complete shade". But it was only after independence, at the very beginning of Singapore's spectactular rise as a city state, that "greening" became a matter of public policy. Concerned about the dehumanizing influence of a concrete jungle, Prime Minister Lee Kuan Yew presciently launched the Garden City concept in 1967, followed by an annual Tree Planting Day in 1971. The concept required vision, determination, education, hard work and money.

But it was done, and is being accomplished still by dedicated city planners, botanists, landscapers, and private residents. Old parks have been restored and new ones planted. The great Botanic Gardens was expanded and took on the task of introducing and testing plants from abroad that would add variety and interest to public landscapes. New attractions like the Zoological Gardens, the Jurong Bird Park, and Sentosa Island incorporated stunning garden plantings as well as their primary exhibits. Most of all, perhaps, non-official Singaporeans have responded to the effort, sometimes creating imaginative gardens of their own in whatever spaces are available to them and also making use of the parks, large and small, that are rarely far from where they live. The results can been seen on the following pages, a tribute to all those who have indeed made Singapore a unique City of Gardens.

CLOVE, PINEAPPLE, GAMBIER, COFFEE, AND PEPPER PLANTATIONS.

beautifu
in the
batum, c
the exqu
purple le
hiding i
and man
Pitche
are by no
oods

and suc
developec
cups, con
by certain
whose de
plant.   T
be quite o
ver

Some Historical Notes

The evolution of Singapore into a city of gardens has been a long process going back over centuries, with the immigration of its plants paralleling the arrival of its varied population. It was influenced by outside forces, notably the search for rare spices by explorers from distant Europe, which in time led to colonization, and also by the changing tastes and interests of those who elected to settle here, most remarkably in the past 40 years.

Though Singapore's history can be traced back to the 14th century, very little is known about its vegetation. What records exist state that the island was covered with thick jungle and had fine timber trees suitable for ship-building. This is unsurprising in view of the fact that Singapore and the Malay Peninsula share the same tropical rainforest and mangrove swamp forest with fringes of coconut trees. Before the first Europeans arrived, there was active trade with China and India and points farther west, as well as links with the vast Indo-Malay Archipelago. By the time Sir Stamford Raffles founded the Settlement in 1819, Malay inhabitants were living in villages near the coast and some Chinese in the interior were cultivating gambier (*Uncaria gambier*) and pepper. Among the trees and plants in the dense jungle that covered the island were some that later gave their Malay names to parts of modern Singapore: Tampines (*Streblus elongatus*) for instance, as well as Kranji (*Dialium*), Tanjong Rhu (*Casuarina*), Katong (*Cynometra malaccensis*) and Tengah (*Ceriops*).

The earliest plant immigrants of which there are extant records and anecdotes were economic crops. Raffles, perhaps fuelled by his own keen interest in natural history, promoted agricultural development as well as trade. In the grounds of the first Government Residence on Fort Canning, then known to the Malays as Bukit Larangan or Forbidden Hill, he planted nutmeg (*Myristica fragrans*), a much-coveted

← Five of the early crops that were tried out in 19th-century Singapore. Clockwise from top left: cloves, pineapples, pepper, coffee and gambier. The cultivation of pineapples endured the longest. Gambier, native to Singaproe, was the earliest agricultural enterprise.

↓ *Piper nigrum*, the source of both 'black' and 'white' pepper was one of the first spices that began the search for the Spice Islands.

↓ ↓ Nutmeg and its companion Mace. *Myristica fragrans* and clove trees were planted by Raffles on Government Hill.

→ *Syzygium malaccensis*, the Malay Apple or *Jumbu bol*. The tree is of medium height, conical in shape with glossy large leaves, large pink showy flowers and bright crimson fruit.

↘ *Lansium domesticum*, the Duku or Langsat, an indigenous fruit that was recorded by the Malay Annals as existing in Singapore in 1819.

↗ Three young fruits of the Jackfruit tree (*Artocarpus heterophyllus*).

↗ ↗ *Durio zebithinus* or the Durian, arguably the most famous fruit in the Malay Archipelago, was recorded as growing on Frobidden Hill at the time of Raffles.

↗ ↗ ↗ *Garcinia mangostana*. A popular fruit, the Mangosteen was once the subject of a clipper race to see who could get the fruit to Queen Victoria first.

→ ↘ The two archival photos show immigrant Chinese farmers in Singapore in 1890 (the group) and 1920 (the single farmer). The former depicts tobacco and pepper crops; in the latter, the farmer is tilling a raised bed which is the traditional way in which fast-growing Chinese leafy vegetables are grown.

↘ *Nephelium lappaceum*. The Rambutan is one of the most attractive of indigenous fruits.

spice that was thought to be native to only five small islands in the Moluccas and some cloves (*Syzygium aromaticum*). When the jungle was cleared to build the Residence on Forbidden Hill, some fruit trees were discovered. The Malay Annals, a 17th-century account of Malay history, state: "In performing this work, they found numbers of fruit trees of all descriptions such as durian trees that two men could barely girth with their arms so extremely old were they. There were also duku trees, orange trees, langsat trees and trees with bad smelling fruit as the *petai* (*Parkia speciosa*) and the *jering* (*Pithecellobium jiringa*)". These are all found today in any domesticated setting in the Malay Peninsula. None, however, is included in the present vegetation on Fort Canning hill, where the only plants that may remain from early times are small like the little creeper Geophila. Its presence was recorded by Charles de Alwis, a botanical artist at the Botanical Gardens who worked at the beginning of the 20th century; it can still be seen growing near the Registry of Muslim marriages on the hill.

From 1836 onwards, when sugar and cotton were introduced for commercial cultivation, many other crops were grown in Singapore. Among these were indigenous plants like gambier and pepper and such introduced ones as nutmeg, coffee, cloves, sugar cane, tobacco and pineapples. Most of the introduced crops eventually failed, either because the soil or the climate was found to be unsuitable or because disease wiped out the enterprise. However, street names still commemorate these early attempts at agriculture: Nutmeg Road, Orange Grove Road, Orchard Road, for example, are very much still in existence, as are D'Almeida Street, Balestier Road, Dunman Road, Oxley Road, Prinsep Street and Scotts Road, all named after the men who tried to cultivate such crops. Here and there in various parts of Singapore, more tangible remains can be found. In a former cemetery in the Bukit Timah district there are two mature nutmeg trees, and in the same area, near the Bukit Timah Nature Reserve, five venerable clove trees grew until they were unfortunately destroyed in the recent construction of a condominium.

These agricultural efforts resulted in the progressive destruction of the native forest. Gambier required firewood to boil the leaves in order to extract the saleable substance; so huge numbers of trees were cut down for fuel. The cultivation of pepper went hand in hand with that of gambier, since once the leaves had been boiled for their extract they were used as an essential fertilizer for the pepper vines.

More land was required for "pineries", commercial smallholdings that grew pineapples. According to a writer in the 1860s, they were the staple fruit for European dinner tables. The pineapple was a notable immigrant from the New World; no one knows who introduced it to Asia, but by 1856 it was a significant crop in Singapore. An account of the agriculture of the Settlement states that it was extensively grown west of the harbour by Bugis people. A Pineapple Industry Ordinance was passed in 1934 to control it and a variety called "Singapore Red" was developed.

↑ ↑ European residence at the end of the 1800s: the type of garden is typical of the time. Note the topiary bush, clipped into the shape of a bird, and the prolific *Antigonon leptopus* growing up to the first floor.

↑ Later European house in the "Black-and-White" style in the Botanic Gardens shows the Talipot palm (*Corypha umbraculifera*), the largest fan palm in the world, in the foreground.

→ European group, 1890s. Their gardens were typically laid out with lawns, hedges and tennis courts.

→ → Photogravure by CJ Kleingrothe depicts the Botanic Gardens road at the end of the 1890s. By this time many plants would have arrived in Singapore through the Botanic Gardens. Photos top left and far right courtesy of Antiques of the Orient.

As the population grew and the town expanded, more permanent houses were built. The homes of European residents are always described as being out of town, spacious and surrounded by gardens, with an abundance of fruit trees. Descriptions of the viands offered at dinner tables list the native rambutan, mangosteen, duku, and banana as well as the exotic pineapple, the papaya, and various kinds of Annonas. These fruit trees were planted after the failure of many of the plantation ventures and as late as the mid-1880s. But ornamental plants, too, were by then part of the scene. With the development of the Settlement from its early frontier town character to a more organized and prosperous town and with the increasing number of women coming to Singapore, the idea of gardening, at least among the European population, had arrived.

Singapore was governed from India until 1867, so it is probable that seeds and cuttings came from there, particularly from Calcutta. Writing in the 1840s, Dr Thomas Oxley lists many ornamentals in local gardens, among them Acacia, Agave, Allamanda, Barleria, Bignonia, Clerodendrum, Crinum, Cassia, Erythrina, Dracaena, assorted Ficus, Gardenia, Hibiscus, Jatropha, Lantana, Murraya, Nerium, Plumbago, Plumeria, Quisqualis, and Yucca – a fine mix of indigenous as well as introduced plants. There was also contact with other tropical botanic gardens, some ruled by powers other than the British. The Calcutta Botanic Garden was under Nathaniel Wallich, a Dane, who was to play an

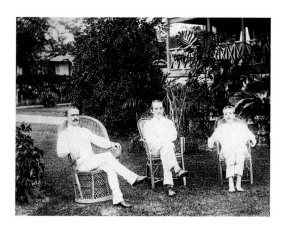

important role in the development of the Singapore Botanic Gardens. Plant species moved unhindered from one colony to another, from East to West, and vice versa. In this way, Singapore received rather early in its modern life a great number of plants that were indigenous to other parts of the world.

The gardens of the Europeans were laid out with lawns, hedges, and tennis courts. James Cameron, an English resident, wrote that the hedges were of Bamboo and wild Heliotrope; the latter was very likely *Duranta repens* or *D. procumbens*, the flowers of which greatly resemble Heliotrope in colour, scent and form. Tennis court fencing was covered by a pale lavender Ipomoea and *Passiflora laurifolia* that grew very quickly. There are no extant garden books or newspaper articles written by English-women in Singapore before the 1950s, but some written earlier in the Malay States display the same longing for the flowers of 'home' and 'homelike' displays as those written by the Memsahibs of India in the days of the Raj. All discuss the kind of flowers that are associated with the English cottage garden that they tried to grow 'out East'. It is not surprising that Dr Oxley's list includes many flowers that are traditionally associated with this style of garden.

↑ All the flowers in this tray are scented except for the lemon yellow Cosmos. All are commonly used for votive offerings and are, clockwise from top left, *Tabernaemontana coronaria*, Vallaris, *Nyctanthes arbor-tristis*, Cosmos, *Hedychium gardenarium* and Plumeria.

→ Ginger, *Zingiber officinalis*. About 400 members of the ginger family grow wild in tropical Asia, but this particular variety is known as ginger.

This feeling of something from 'home' is also displayed by the Chinese, Indian and Indonesian immigrants who came to Singapore over the years. Immigrant communities very often carry with them plants, seeds or cuttings of two major kinds. The first of these, almost always scented, are votive plants used in rituals, as offerings to deities, as 'good luck' plants and on ceremonial occasions. Among them is *Nyctanthes arbor-tristis*, the 'Sad Tree', a native Indian tree which forms part of Hindu and Buddhist ritual offerings. The scented flowers are white and coral and bloom at night; by the dawn they have 'wept' onto the ground where devout ladies gather them for votive offerings. In Singapore it can be found in the Hindu and Buddhist temples in Ceylon Road and St Michael's Road. A shrub or small tree native to South China, *Aglaia odorata* is often planted in front of Chinese houses together with *Platycladus orientalis*. Both are 'good luck' plants, always placed side by side. Aglaia has minute yellow flowers that in the past were used to scent tobacco and was once called the 'tobacco flower'. Platycladus is a cypress, the lace-like fronds of which are placed within the gifts exchanged at Cantonese weddings by the bride and groom's families. A plant common to both Indian and Chinese cultures is Nelumbium, the lotus. Plumeria, the frangipani, a Mexican native, arrived in Singapore via an unknown intermediate source. It, too, is used in temple offerings. Other sweet-scented votive flowers include *Michelia champaca*, *Michelia figo* and Vallaris, the latter being a favourite of Peranakan Nonyas (Straits-born Chinese women).

The second group of plants carried by immigrants consisted of those used for food and medicine. The Neem tree, *Azadiracta indica*, a veritable pharma-coepia by itself, came early to the Malay Peninsula from India. Ginger, *Zingiber officinalis*, so ancient in use that its place of origin is unknown, is used for both purposes, as is coriander and turmeric. Other introduced culinary herbs include lemon grass (*Cymbopogon citratus*), from South India, and various rhizomes and leaves of the Curcuma family.

← *Saracca taipingensis*. Named after the town in Malaysia where it was first recorded, this is a leguminous tree that flowers in flushes with large masses of flowers that are the delight of bees. Large seed pods follow. The flowers range from a pale mustard colour to a deeper orange in different varieties.

↙ Nelumbium, the lotus, a flower associated with many religions and which appears in art, food and architecture.

↓ *Duranta repens* or *D. procumbens*. Wrongly identified in the early days of Singapore as Heliotrope, an understandable error as it closely resembles the Heliotrope. It has sweetly scented flowers, followed by golden trusses of berries.

Gardens of the past reflected these ethnic tastes. The more well-off Chinese, particularly the Peranakans, had spacious houses by the seaside in the Katong district. A characteristic feature of these homes were plants in large, decorative Chinese clay or porcelain pots, in which were planted, according to the fashion of the day, Adeniums (native to the dry climate of Aden) or Spathoglottis (native to the Malay archipelago). The bright-yellow Oncidium "Golden Shower", a local hybrid, also enjoyed a great vogue.

The Indian population tended to live in town or on rural estates in the interior, and plants with an especially Indian character were to be found around their homes. Among these were the drumstick tree (*Moringa oleifera*), various gourds for the Indian vegetarian diet, and the curry leaf (*Murraya koenigii*), *Piper betele*, the masticatory leaf, as well as such ornamentals as Tabernaemontana and marigold (for offerings) and a crimson rose of unknown origin, also used by Malays who call it the *Bunga mawar*. This is the only rose that grows easily in Singapore. It is fully double with a strong sweet scent and has been used to make rose syrup. Rose syrup forms part of a non alcoholic drink popular among Muslims when mixed with milk called *Syrup Bandung*.

The middle classes of all ethnicities had similar gardens with a patch of lawn, flowering shrubs, bamboo clumps, or cannas in island beds or planted along driveways, perhaps an orchid enclosure or fern house. There were vogues for various plants from time to time, very much as happens in garden circles today. Pink, lavender, and white forms of Spathoglottis, planted along driveways, were popular up until the 1950s when a craze for the yellow form from the Philippines arrived. *Heliconia psittacorum*, called Japanese canna even up to the 1950s, was common in the 1930s, as were hedges of the 'shoe flower' (*Hibiscus rosa-sinensis*), a thin bamboo, *Hymenocallis crinum* and the salmon-coloured Hippeastrum. All homes also had their kitchen herbs and plants. The Singapore Gardening Society aroused a greater interest in ornamental plants and nurseries were established to cater to it.

For the rest of the population – town dwellers living in cramped and crowded conditions – the basic need in some people to grow things was manifested by plants housed haphazardly in whatever domestic utensil came to hand. These plants comprised herbs used in traditional medicine such as *Plectranthus amboinicus*; *Punica granatum* (small pomegranate trees), limes, pandan leaves (*Pandanus amaryllifolius*), and small edible herbs such as the Tallinum were commonly seen. They were a mixture of the utilitarian and the ornamental.

The Malay population tended to live by the coast among coconut trees in kampongs. These were characterized by houses raised on stilts, with the surrounding area swept cleanly but with essential food plants like the banana growing nearby. The Betel Nut Palm, *Pandanus amaryllifolius*, lemon grass (*Cymbopogon citratus*) and tapioca were common, as were the odd clump of sugar cane and herbs and plants traditionally used in the Malay *materia medica*.

As early as the 1840s, Chinese farmers who lived in the rural areas supplied the population with an astonishing variety of vegetables. The list includes numerous gourds and melons, spinach, onions and garlic, radish and sweet potatoes. Dr Oxley reported success with European varieties such as cabbage, lettuce, parsnips and tomatoes. Chinese market gardeners continued to grow vegetables in the traditional organic way until well into the 1960s.

↖ ← Two traditional and typical Malay houses. The postcard depicts a house in the 19th century, and the photograph, a house that existed up to the 1960s. Both show a cleanswept area adjacent to the house with similar planting. Trees (at top) include coconuts, a banana on right and a *Tamarindus indica* at centre. The other house is situated in a coconut orchard; there are also bananas and a pair of *Chrysalidocarpus lutescens*, the Yellow palm.

↗ Part of Whampoa's garden showing a tiled "moon gate" with large pots containing a pair of topiary pagodas with the dog of *Fo* on the top.

→ Magenta Cottage, a house in the Anglo-Chinese style, shows the formal nature of the garden of the successful Chinese resident of old Singapore. Glazed, ornamental pots line the driveway. Two photos on right courtesy of Antiques of the Orient

Singapore was not noted for large private gardens of distinction. An exception was the 19th-century garden of Hoo Ah Kay, known as Whampoa (see previous page), a prosperous Chinese merchant famed for his hospitality and generosity. All the commentators on life in Singapore of that period mention and praise this garden, which boasted a *Victoria amazonica* (known as *V. regia* in the heyday of empire), the horticultural marvel of the day. Other European and more prosperous Asian residents must also have had gardens that demonstrated taste and skill, but they were neither photographed nor recorded. Such photographs as are available are usually not of the garden per se but rather of a family function or some notable event. Still, the Governor of the Straits Settlements, Sir Shenton Thomas, probably had private gardens in mind when he opened a flower show in 1939 and said: "It seems to me that during my time here there has been a considerable increase in the variety, and a noticeable improvement in the quality, of the flowers and plants that one sees in the gardens and nurseries; and in this development both amateurs and Chinese nursery gardeners have played a note-worthy part. Singapore is becoming very much a city of gardens, a delight both to those who live in it and to those who visit it. The love of flowers never did anyone any harm, and in these troublous days it is a comfort and a relaxation to get away into one's garden, to gaze at one's small successes, to ponder over the failures, and to plan better for the future. In this we can all learn from one another, whatever our position or race."

↖ ← Tanjong Katong and Katong were two of the more popular richer districts. The two houses by the sea (at top) from the 1930s have tall coconut trees with wide lawns leading down to the beach. Shrubs and flowers (such as shown here) were usually planted on the landward side away from the salt spray. The postcard below depicts the Sea View Hotel.

→ These photos from the 1940s show a house inland in the Serangoon area near the former sand pits. There are several *Casuarina equisetifolia* trees, on the right a huge mass of the original Singapore Beauty Bougainvillea, with planting along the driveway again in individual pots, this time with a mixture of Yellow palm and Oncidium.

→ The Swiss Club dates from the 1920s. Here is a view of its verandah restaurant, a later addition to the main building. Designed to look out over the garden, one has the feeling of eating outdoors.

↓ A "Black-and-White" house on Nassim Road, framed by an old Mango tree. The stairs leading to the first floor are behind the latticed woodwork. The main living quarters where socializing and domestic activities took place was on the upper floor, where vistas of the garden were paramount.

→ → The *porte-cochère* of a typical colonial residence. A balustrade planted with Bird's Nest Ferns lines the driveway.

Colonial Era Houses and House Gardens

Away from the city centre, along winding roads lined with venerable trees can be seen some of the elegant residences dating from Singapore's colonial period. Many of these were built in the 1910s and 1920s in Mock Tudor or "Black-and-White" style, with elevated verandahs and spacious rooms, but some date from the late 1800s. Often they were built on former plantations, as in Goodwood Hill, Gallop Road and Adam Park. Here, the houses were not separated by hedges or fences and the landscaping was characterized by sweeping parks with clumps of trees planted so as to afford pleasant views from the verandahs. Few had notable gardens; generally, a large lawn and a few trees sufficed, with perhaps a bed or two of easy-to-maintain Cannas and Hibiscus. Today, not much has changed, but even with such minimal planting, the sheer size of the gardens makes them impressive.

← An impressive private driveway sweeps up to the columned portico of this late 19th-century house called Tilton; plantings that include Ixora and *Chrysalidocarpus lutescens* line the drive.

→ Frank Brewer-designed Arts and Crafts style house in Dalvey Estate with exposed brickwork and arches has the same style of garden it probably would have had in the 1920s when it was laid out. A few mature trees and some Traveller's palms set in a sweeping lawn would have been considered sufficient landscaping. An *Elaeis guineensis* palm is on the right.

→ Eden Hall, now the residence of the British High Commissioner, was built in about 1912 in the Grand Manner. Designed by Swan & Maclaren, it is an imposing structure. Such houses would have had trees closely planted along the perimeters of the property and (if room permitted) further clumps of trees set within the lawns. The native Tembusu (*Fagraea fragrans*) was a favorite in the Tanglin area where this house is situated. Nearer the house flowering shrubs would have been planted. Note the stand of Manila palms at centre; these would have been a relatively recent addition to the grounds.

← Early "Black-and-White" house on Goodwood Hill, approached by a drive lined with a row of "lollipop" Bougainvillea. The upper-floor verandah on left is open on three sides and represents the ultimate in tropical living. Designed to catch the breeze and offer views of the garden, it is connected to the other rooms upstairs by a cantilevered balcony. It offered a fine view of the numerous epiphytes growing on the trees.

The Istana Gardens

Located near the end of Orchard Road in the heart of the city, guarded by splendid wrought-iron gates, the Istana (which means "palace" in Malay) stands on what was once a Nutmeg plantation. The government acquired the site in 1865, by which time disease had destroyed the nutmeg trees, and erected a two-storey residence with classic Corinthian, Doric, and Ionic features, overlooking extensive grounds that now include sweeping lawns, ponds, and a nine-hole golf course. Twenty-one British governers lived in this building, which since independence has been the official residence of Singapore's President.

The formal gardens around the residence occupy an area of 18,200 square metres and have recently undergone an extensive restoration, adding over 125 new botanical species to the 51 species of shrubs, 51 species of ornamental trees, and 25 species of fruit trees already growing on the site.

← The elegant facade of the Istana, nestling in a sea of greenery.

↑ *Bauhinia kockiana*, a colourful creeper native to the jungles of Malaysia, has been trained over trellises surrounding the central fountain. Benches are set below for visitors to rest in the shade.

↗ A stairway leads down from the parade area to a terraced area, with a view of Singapore's modern skyscrapers beyond.

→ A water feature set within a circular lawn used for garden parties was recently installed in 1996 when the gardens were thoroughly replanted.

Some 45 species of birds also make their home in this restful expanse of greenery. A stroll through the Istana gardens provides a comprehensive survey of Singapore's botanic history, both commercial and ornamental. Near the Spice Terrace, for example, can be found aromatic clove trees and some of the original nutmegs, both widely grown in the early years. Around Swan Pond, a 150-metre long water feature, grow such palms as Livistona, Caryota, Ptychosperma, and the indigenous *Ptycoraphis Singaporensis*, as well as tall trees like Albizzia, Eugenia, Purple Milletia, and African Mahogany. Jungle trees include the tall Tembusu, the dome-shaped Jelutong (*Dyera costulata*), and the yellow-blooming Saraca.

The front area of the Istana has been planted in the style of a cottage garden, using some 50 flowering shrubs to create a variety of colour and texture. Directly adjacent the parade ground, the palette is of red, oranges and yellows with such species as Golden Thrysalis, Ixora and Lantana. Further down in the area reserved for functions around the water feature, the "blue zone" incorporating such plants as Plumbago and Angelonia is a cool combination of mauves, blues and purples. As one descends, the colour scheme pales into shades of pink with rows of Singapore's national flower the Vanda Miss Joaquim set amidst hedges of Tibouchina.

↖ A Rain tree shades the entrance to the Istana.

↖ The Sri Temasek building, with distinctive architectural influence from the Malay house. The lattice work below the eaves was decorative, but also served as a rain drip, which when in contact with the wind cooled those sitting on the verandah.

← A pool of aquatic plants stretches to a gazebo sheltering a white marble statue of Queen Victoria that once stood in the ballroom. It was presented to Her Majesty by the town's Chinese population on the occasion of her Golden Jubilee.

→ A photogravure taken by Charles J Kleingrothe *circa* 1900 that shows the landscape in the extensive park admirably. On left is an *Arucaria heterophylla* or Norfolk Pine, with a Yucca below. The palm planted at centre is an *Arenga pinnata*. Photo courtesy of Antiques of the Orient.

The Padang and Esplanade Park

Overlooked by such survivors of the colonial period as City Hall, the Victoria Memorial Hall, and the Supreme Court, the Padang has been the scene of many historic events. Here, in what was then a dense jungle, Raffles first raised the British flag. Later it became the city's sporting and social center, when the broad field was used for cricket, rugby and lawn bowls and the Singapore Cricket Club, founded in 1852, served as an exclusive gathering place for the rulers. In the dark days of 1942 most of those rulers, including women and children, were assembled here by the victorious Japanese and marched off to prison camps from which many failed to return. Crowds massed on the field on September 12, 1945, to watch Lord Louis Mountbatten receive the Japanese surrender on the steps of City Hall and again in 1965 to celebrate the emergence of a fully independent Singapore.

The Padang remains an expanse of green close to the towering business district. Looking much as it did in the past, its surrounding pavements are lined with Rain trees along Connaught Drive. As in the past, it is used for most of the republic's big sporting events; at one end lies the clubhouse (1884) of the Singapore Cricket Club, at the other, the Singapore Recreation Club.

More greenery can be found in Esplanade Park, constructed on reclaimed land just southwest of the Padang. Here among the sights in tree-dotted lawns stands the memorial to those who died in both World Wars, as well as another to a Chinese hero named Lim Bo Seng, who fought as a guerilla against the Japanese as part of the famed Force 136 and who was tortured to death after his capture. From here you can look across the mouth of the Singapore River to the 8-m (26-ft) tall statue of the merlion (1972) – a national symbol created by the Singapore Tourism Board (see page 2).

← An early photograph of the Padang. Cricket was played here from 1837.

↑↑ The towers of modern Singapore's financial center rise above the Cricket Club, which dates from 1852.

↑ Old painting of the Padang at the turn of the century, showing Angsana trees (*Pterocarpus indicus*) introduced from Malacca. Photos on left and above courtesy of Antiques of the Orient.

→ The Cenotaph, unveiled in 1922 by the Prince of Wales as a memorial to those killed in World War I. Planted around it are a number of Coral Trees (*Erythrina glauca*), a tree often planted in Singapore's parks for its mass of beautiful scarlet flowers.

↑ Victoria Memorial Hall, framed by *Peltophorum pterocarpum* trees was built in 1905 in memory of the former Queen. Now comprising the Victoria Concert Hall and Victoria Theatre, concerts and other performances are regularly held here.

↗ The Supreme Court, constructed in 1937–39, the last Classical building to be erected in Singapore; it was formally opened by Sir Shenton Thomas, a previous governor.

→ The Lim Bo Seng Memorial in Esplanade Park, built in 1954 to mark the tenth anniversary of the death of the Chinese resistance fighter killed by the Japanese during World War II.

Raffles Hotel

Raffles Hotel is a hallowed Singapore institution, more famous perhaps than any of the others named after the settlement's founder. It began in 1887 as a modest ten-room guest house which was taken over by the Sarkies brothers, Armenian emigrants who had already launched the Eastern & Oriental Hotel in Penang and who would later build the Strand in Rangoon. Two years later Rudyard Kipling came for dinner and wrote, "Let the traveller take note. Feed at Raffles and sleep at the Hotel de l'Europe." The owners also took note; within a few years they had added a whole complex of new buildings connected by courtyards, and had transformed Raffles into one of the best-known hotels in the Orient. By the late 1970s, however, its glamorous reputation could no longer disguise the fact that Raffles was getting old. In the year of its centenary it was declared a National Monument and then extensively restored.

← A deep, cool verandah overlooks a courtyard in one wing, offering a view of Plumeria trees, Heliconia, and a neatly-trimmed lawn.

→ Entrance courtyard of Raffles. The Traveller's Palm growing on the right has become an emblem of the hotel and appears on countless old postcards. Variegated Pandanus makes an attractive ground cover below.

→ An ornate cast-iron fountain brings the cooling sound of water to one of the courtyards. It was imported from Glasgow in 1890, and was donated to the hotel by a local family .

→ → Red tiling accents the lush greenery of the Fern Court, where a more contemporary feeling is created.

↓ The private Palm Court, reserved for hotel guests, is a simple, formal garden consisting mainly of *Livistona rotundifolia* palms and grass. A pink Plumeria adds a touch of colour.

The Raffles gardens today are an imaginative recreation of the past. They contain over 50,000 different plants with 80 species and are tended by a resident horticulturalist and six full-time gardeners. Almost an emblem are the stately Traveller's Palms (*Ravenala madagascariensis*) which grow outside the main entrance and in several of the interior gardens. Equally nostalgic are the lofty palms and fragrant Plumeria trees around the Palm Court, perhaps the most famous of the gardens which dates back to the 19th century. Most of the 14-m-tall *Livistona rotundifolia* palms are the originals and they were carefully protected during the restoration, as were the white and pink Plumeria trees. A jungle-type planting can be seen in the Fern Court, where Oil Palms (*Elaeis guineesis*) and Ficus trees rise out of a mass of bananas, Bird's Nest Ferns and gingers.

←← Bras Basah Park, with Rain trees (*Samanea saman*), among the most popular of Singapore's wayside trees.

← The Singapore History Museum, formerly known as the Raffles Museum, opened in 1996 in its new incarnation. Surrounded by trees and some small lawns, it has an interesting sculpture of visitors sitting on a bench at the entrance.

↓ Forecourt of the National Art Museum, formerly St Joseph's Institution, a school for boys run by the Christian Brothers of John Baptist de la Salle. Built in 1867 and expanded several times, it was converted to an art gallery at the end of the 1990s. In the foreground may be seen the ubiquitous *Heliconia psittacorum* and the stately *Roystonia regia* palms.

Bras Basah Park

Bras Basah (Brass Bassa is the spelling on an 1835 map) means "wet rice" in Malay, and the park and street that bear this name were once part of a low-lying area watered by a stream, along which rice was laid out to dry. Located at the entrance to the Civic District, the park was redeveloped in 1983–84 and now consists of a broad flat expanse of grass shaded by such flowering trees as *Tabebuia pallida*, *Lagerstroemia speciosa*, and *Samanea saman*. It is one of the largest green areas in the old part of Singapore, and used to be the site of the Ladies' Lawn Tennis Club.

Around it are a number of the city's cultural centers, housed in historic buildings, among them the Asian Heritage Museum, the Singapore History Museum and the National Art Museum. St Andrews Cathedral, which can be seen from the park, was built between 1856–61 on the site of two earlier churches and was designated as a national monument in 1973.

Fort Canning Park

Fort Canning is one of the oldest sites in Singapore. Archaeological excavations have revealed that the hill was the seat of the Malay kingdom of Temasek in the 14th century, chosen – so legend claims – because on it the ruler saw what he took to be a lion and thus named the island Singapura (Lion City). The kingdom was gone by the time Sir Stamford Raffles arrived in 1819, but Malays still called the hill Bukit Larangan or "Forbidden Hill" and believed it to be haunted. Undeterred, Raffles built his first bungalow there and laid out the first botanical garden of spice trees on its slopes. Governors of Singapore lived on the hill until the mid-19th century, when it became a fort named after Viscount Charles John Canning, first Viceroy of India. It served as a military base until the 1970s when the National Parks Board began the process of turning it into a public park, with spacious lawns, recreation facilities, and a spice garden.

↑ Fort Canning Centre at the top of the hill, built in 1926 as a barracks for the British Army; recently renovated, it is used today for various cultural events.

→ Government Hill was fortified between 1856 to 1861 with the addition of the fort, officers' quarters and several 68-pound canons that overlooked the town and harbour. From this vantage point one may still see the now-modern city stretching out below.

→ → Fort Canning Gate. This and an adjoining wall inset with gravestones are all that remain of an old cemetery on the site.

← A drive in the park shaded by Ficus and other large trees. An Indian Laburnum (*Cassia fistula*), also known as the Golden Shower tree because of its bright flowers, can be seen in the distance.

→ The Spice Garden with lemon grass (*Cymbopogon citratus*) and pandan (*Pandanus amaryllifolius*) in the foreground, bilimbing (*Averrhoa belimbi*) and clove trees (*Syzygium aromatica*) behind.

↘ When the Park was redeveloped, the cemetery graves were exhumed and the tombstones were set in one area as a memorial of some of Singapore's early residents; the inscriptions provide a poignant glimpse of the hazards of life in this outpost in the 19th century.

Chijmes

CHIJMES, the popular acronym for the Convent of the Holy Infant Jesus occupies a block in what was once the center of the Catholic Church mission schools. It includes a number of buildings, some dating back nearly a century and a half. The nucleus was Caldwell House (1841); designed by George Coleman, it was once a private residence and later served as the Catholic girls' school. The second oldest building was an orphanage, while the most imposing is a Gothic-style chapel designed in the 1890s by French priest, Charles Benedict Nain. In redeveloping the property for commercial use, care was taken to maintain the various buildings and the chapel was carefully preserved. A large area of lawn in the central upper level hosts open-air concerts and theatrical events, while palms, small trees and blooming displays of Bougainvillea are planted on both the upper and lower levels, bringing a welcome touch of tropical green to the downtown area.

← Central court at the Chijmes complex features *Dalbergia oliveri* trees and a large lawn.

↑ The Gothic-style chapel has been deconsecrated and is now used for various functions. Containers overlooking the interior courtyard are planted with Bougainvillea.

→ *Veitchia merrillii* palms line the pathways in front of the cloistered walls of one of the Chijmes buildings. The whole complex has been designated a National Monument.

Istana Park

Facing the entrance of the Istana, on the opposite side of Orchard Road, this is a high-profile park in a distinctive position within the city. It has undergone a number of restorations over the years, the most recent revamp being under the direction of Ren Matsui as design consultant. Tall, stylized gates, and a row of flag-poles have been installed over a large reflecting pool on one side. These symbolize the park's situation as the gateway to the Civic District, as well as its proximity to the Istana. There is also a waterside restaurant that was created in order to encourage people to use the green spaces provided by the National Parks Board. The rest of the park offers a lush display of tropical green with such palms as Fishtail (*Caryota mitis*), Assai (*Euterpe edulis*) and Rhapis rising among numerous flowering trees, while varied ferns and Philodendrons thrive in shady areas. Colour is provided by beds of Heliconia, Anthurium and assorted foliage plants.

↑ Ever-blooming *Heliconia psittacorum* in one of the park's sunny beds.

← A Licuala palm in full fruit and a giant fern (*Cyathea* sp) add to the luxuriant atmosphere.

→ Pathways lead through beds of varied ornamentals; on the right are the large leaves of a self-heading *Philodenron selloum*, below which Spathiphyllum and Anthurium form an exotic ground cover.

Suntec City

Suntec City, opened in 1995, is one of the newest additions to Singapore's downtown area. The largest privately-owned development in the city, it includes the vast International Convention and Exhibition Centre as well as five tall office buildings, various entertainment facilities and the city's largest shopping complex. It is part of an ambitious project known as Marina Bay, the other two sections being Marina Square and Millennium Walk (see pages 58–59), all rising on 84 hectares of reclaimed land. Two five-star luxury hotels, the Ritz Carlton and the Conrad International, are also part of the complex, making it possible for convention delegates to work and enjoy themselves within a fairly limited area.

Reflecting the work of some of the world's leading contemporary architects – Philip Johnson, Kevin Roche and John Burges all contributed to aspects of Marina Bay – the complex boasts the latest in

↑ Green trees soften the effect of Singapore's soaring new skyline.

→ A courtyard in Suntec City, where young *Delonix regia* (Flame of the Forest) are planted in beds covered by low-growing *Wedelia trilobata*.

→ → Facing the cutting-edge Convention and Exhibition Centre are a number of impressive *Khaya grandifolia* or African Mahogany trees. Brought to Singapore from tropical Africa, they grow to more than 30 m in height, and thus blend well with tall buildings in city settings. In the foreground on left the fan palms are Livistona, while the taller single one is a *Roystonia regia*.

cutting-edge design and technology; but is firmly rooted in the Chinese art of geomancy or *feng shui*. The name Suntec is derived from the characters "xin da" which translates as "new achievement". Its buildings and features are arranged to create harmony and attract good fortune. Viewed from above, the five office towers resemble a hand – the 18-storey Suntec City Tower represents the thumb, the four 45-storey office towers the fingers, the Convention and Exhibition Centre the wrist, while the fountain plaza is like a gold ring placed in the centre of the palm.

The complex also incorporates many open spaces and the touches of green on which modern Singapore prides itself. One courtyard is transformed into a small forest of flowering trees, while an area connecting two buildings is a luxuriant blend of trees, palms, creepers and flowering shrubs; even an escalator is lushly planted down its entire length.

← Supported by four 13.8-m-high bronze legs and spreading over an area of 1683 m, the Fountain of Wealth has been accorded the status of "World's Largest Fountain" in the Guinness Book of Records (1998). Circling the Plaza are 12 bronze medallions depicting the 12 signs of the Chinese Zodiac. It is believed that walking round the fountain will bring energy and luck. Facing the Fountain Plaza are a row of *Bauhinia blakeana* or Hong Kong Bauhinia trees, perhaps planted to pay tribute to the Hong Kong developers.

↑ A *Hopea odorata* tree and *Cyrtostachys renda* palms decorate a walkway.

→ Even escalators are planted with Licuala palms and assorted ornamentals.

Millennium Walk

Part of the Marina Bay project and adjacent to
Suntec City, this is a dramatic shopping mall.
During the day, soft light floods down through 15
lofty asymmetrical pyramids, which are illuminated
by night. While planting is limited mostly to a few
outside expanses of lawn, there is no shortage of
impressive hardscape features such as water flowing
over an intriguingly textured wall, colorful swirling
modern sculptures, and the distinctive shape of
the pyramids. The Ritz Carlton and Conrad
International hotels overlook Millennium Walk.

← Varying textures provide
a dramatic effect on this
water feature; the pyramids
of Millennium Walk can be
seen in the background.

→ Six contemporary
sculptures in bold colors
representing Chinese
characters are by Roy
Lichtenstein; they echo the
curving lines of a raised
lawn outside the mall.

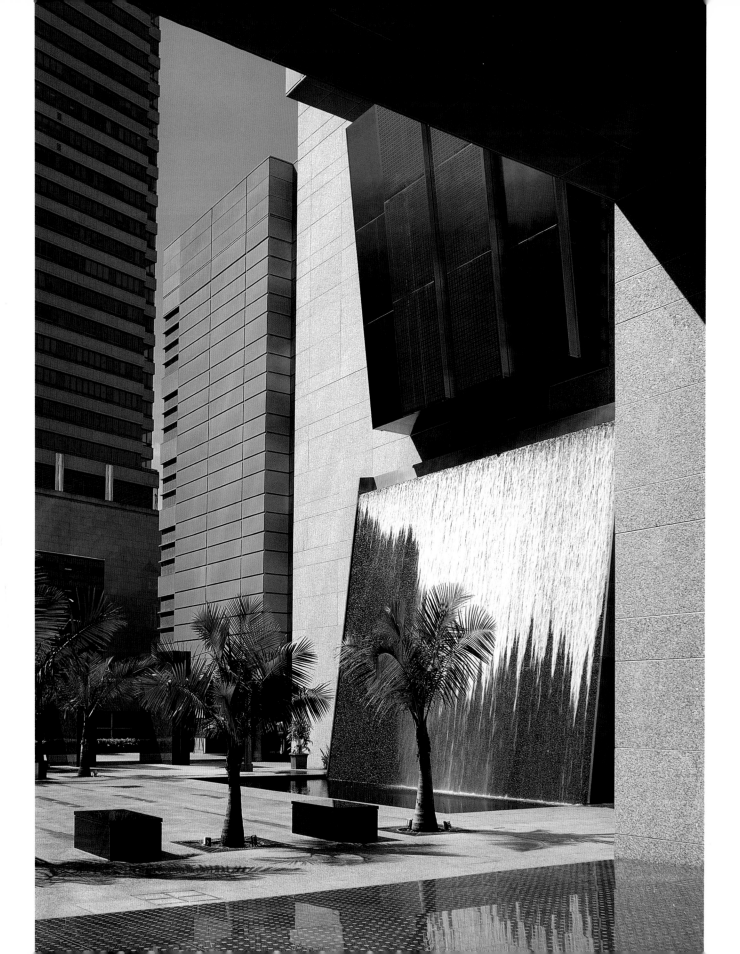

City Courtyards

Downtown Singapore, nearly all of it built on reclaimed land at the point where the Singapore River flows into the sea, is a dazzling display of high-rise buildings, luxury hotels and shopping centers. Gazing at the spectacle from Mount Faber, the writer Jan Morris found the effect "very rich, very arrogant, very vulgar" and felt that she was seeing "something new in the world: the city-state, within its island ramparts, brazen and self-assured."

Heartless as it may look from afar, a closer look at this concentration of glass and cement reveals a gentler, more human side in the form of unexpected green courtyards, dramatic water features and works of art to soothe the spirits of both those who work here and also visiting tourists. In some places the planting has been done by the National Parks Board, in others by the owners of the buildings with horticultural advice from the Board.

← ← An impressive water feature in Capital Square. Designed in 1997 by a US company called Wet Design, the minimalistic planting adds to the modern atmosphere of this outdoor area.

↑ Towers of water flank the Water Gate leading into Far East Square; columns of water shoot up at regular intervals.

← A very controlled, contemporary mini-park created in raised containers near China Place; Hymenocallis, Lantana and Ixora are among the low-growing plants used here.

Far East Square, opened in 1999, incorporates both original and new buildings. Its idea is to recreate the atmosphere of old Chinatown in an area covering 200,000 square feet. Along with restaurants and coffee bars, it contains shops selling traditional Chinese goods, a museum displaying artefacts of early immigrants and the Chui Eng Free School, founded in 1854 as one of Singapore's first free educational institutions. Four gates – named after fire, metal, wood and water – lead into the square; at the latter towers of water and steam rise to provide a periodic display. Plantings are minimal, but there are changing displays of various art pieces.

Another open area is Capitol Square. Here the effect is starkly modernistic, the dominant feature a wall of shimmering water that falls into a plain rectangular reflecting pool with only a few palm trees to suggest the tropical setting. More green can be found in the courtyard at China Place, where a series of raised planter beds contain shade-giving trees like the Yellow Flame (*Peltophorum pterocarpum*) as well as Fan palms and flowering shrubs.

← The low Chinese shop-houses and planting of Far East Square provide a restful contrast to the surrounding towers of glass and cement. *Hopea odorata* trees provide a touch of green.

↗ One of the modern art works in Far East Square provided by a company called Volume and Form.

→ A fountain in a court-yard of Far East Square called the "Spring of Happiness" bubbles up near contemporary sculptures.

↓ → *Bauhinia purpurea*, popularly known as the Orchid tree, is often planted along Chinatown streets.

↓ ↓ An Angsana tree is planted in front of a brightly painted row of houses.

→ → A jackfruit tree (*Artocarpus heterophyllus*) along with Foxtail palms, Cordylines and assorted ornamentals in raised planter boxes in front of two recently restored shophouses in Club Street. Such backgrounds are often used for wedding photos.

Chinatown

Chinatown, southwest of the Singapore River, was part of the town plan laid out by Raffles, divided into areas according to Chinese provinces where the new immigrants had originated. It quickly began to fill during the second half of the 19th century and became virtually a world of its own, occasionally visited by tourists but largely left alone by the British authorities. After independence, as better housing became available elsewhere on the island, it sank into decline and seemed doomed to modern redevelopment. It was saved, at least partially, by the efforts of preservationists who saw its fading buildings as a valuable part of Singapore's cultural heritage. Today many of the old pastel-coloured shophouses and terrace houses have been restored, enhanced by sidewalk plantings, and the area is also linked to city parks by landscaped walkways and cycle paths named by the National Parks Board park connectors.

Orchard Road

Orchard Road's fame as Singapore's busiest shopping centre is relatively recent. In the 1840s, it was devoted largely to Nutmeg and Pepper plantations and was regarded as remote from the town's real life; a tiger was seen there in 1846. In fact, it remained a country lane until the end of the 19th century when increased urbanization resulted in the construction of shophouses, and later larger buildings such as apartment blocks, along its borders. However, it was not until the 1960s, when CK Tang opened a shop at Orchard and Scotts Road, did the area lose its suburban atmosphere. Most of the stately Angsana trees (*Pterocarpus indicus*) that provide welcome shade for today's shoppers date from this period. In addition to such trees, there are a number of pocket parks and imaginative roadside plantings along Orchard, all designed and maintained by the National Parks Board. Despite today's congestion, it still retains its green.

← ← A line of Angsana trees in front of the twin towers of Ngee Ann City and Wisma Atria, two of Orchard Road's famous shopping malls.

↑ Ground cover of Scindapsus complements this modernist sculpture outside Paragon shopping centre.

← In addition to the green, there are some impressive hardscapes along Orchard. The fountain forecourt of Ngee Ann City regularly hosts events on weekends for busy shoppers.

↑ ↗ Shady trees provide welcome respite for shoppers and the plethora of open-air coffee shops that are a relatively recent addition to the area.

→ Glass and chrome entrance to the Mass Rapid Transit system or subway is imaginatively planted with Alexandra palms (*Archontophoenix alexandrae*), a recent introduction from eastern Australia, Heliconias and other ornamentals.

→ → At the top of Orchard Road where it meets Orange Grove Road a pathway is luxuriant with Cordylines, variegated Pandanus and a mass of flowering Hymenocallis.

Many of Singapore's four- and five-star hotels are located in the Orchard Road area; here we showcase two high-altitude gardens of the Grand Hyatt and the famous Shangri-La hotel garden. The Grand Hyatt had little space for a conventional, ground-level garden, so decided to install one on the fourth floor of its Grand Wing tower and another on the fifth floor of its Terrace Wing. The former was conceptualized by Australian-born Made Wijaya, who made his reputation creating memorable gardens in Bali, and executed by his Singapore partner Fairuz Bin Salleh; the latter was designed by Hawaiian Landscapes, an American company. The garden of the Shangri-La hotel, originally designed in 1971 by the American firm of Belt Collins and Associates and recently upgraded, was a pioneering example of how landscape could be integrated with architecture in a tropical setting. Bougainvilleas cascade from balconies, and atrium plantings include tree ferns (Cyathea) along a walkway that leads up a hillside, and stepped masses of Spathiphyllum, Cordylines, and Bird's Nest Ferns.

↖ The 13-m Regency Falls plunge down from the Terrace Wing of the Grand Hyatt, through a dense planting of hardy palms and ferns. Beneath it is an ingeniously hidden multi-storey carpark. Variegated leaved Bougainvillea and *Caesalpina pulcherrima* provide some colour.

← ← A hand-carved pergola in the Grand Hyatt's Grand Tower planting. An open area provides enough sunlight for flowering shrubs here.

← The Shangri-La waterfall spilling down through a mass of rocks and ferns.

→ → Coconut and Areca palms predominate by the Shangri-La pool area.

Emerald Hill

What is now fashionable Emerald Hill, just a short walk from the modern shopping emporia of Orchard Road, was once a nutmeg plantation established in 1837. When that fell victim to a blight that killed most of the island's Nutmeg trees, it passed through various owners during the 19th century until finally, starting in 1902, it became the site of a collection of terrace-style houses for wealthy Straits-born Chinese. Though built by a variety of architects, including at least one Englishman, and displaying both Chinese and European features, the pastel-colored houses today present a harmonious atmosphere, recalling an era that has vanished in many other parts of Singapore.

Emerald Hill owes its continued existence to the Urban Redevelopment Authority, which in 1981 designated it one of Singapore's first conservation projects. Though some of the terrace houses had already been torn down, many were saved and have been lovingly restored. Due to space limitations, such terrace houses rarely have much in the way of gardens, though a few manage mini-jungles with small trees, bananas, and so on. Others have opted for container gardens, arranged so as to create an effect of massed plantings and sometimes changed for such events as Chinese New Year. Hidden from public view, some have small interior courtyards filled with ferns and other plants.

←← An ornamental pediment leads into an intimate courtyard. Such gates would have been later additions.

↙↙ The Bottlebrush tree (*Callistemon* sp) was introduced from Australia to Singapore during the 1990s. These medium-sized trees are often used for lining narrow roads; their cascading branches and bright red flowers are very attractive.

→ In this residence, the Chinese influence of the architecture is complemented by the choice of Bamboo as an ornamental in the front courtyard.

↘ The inner courtyards or light-wells in shophouse architecture provided much-needed ventilation into the long, narrow interiors. Today, they may also provide a touch of green; here a banana (*Musa* sp) graces the area next to a circular iron staircase.

→→ Indoor courtyard decorated with various specimens of potted plants. The pink-flowering one (at centre) is an Adenium; also known as the Japanese Frangipani it is from the same botanical family as the Frangipani. Native to arid East Africa and Arabia, it does best in damp southeast Asia in a sunny location in a well-drained pot.

The Botanic Gardens

Like a number of the world's great botanic gardens – Kew, for instance, in England, and the Longwood Gardens in the United States – the Singapore Botanic Gardens started out solely as a place for aesthetic and recreational enjoyment. Raffles, as we have seen, experimented with a garden of commercial plants – mostly spice trees – around his bungalow on Government Hill in the early 19th century; this barely survived his departure from the island, nor did another, started on the hill by a group called the Agri-Horticultural Society and devoted primarily to Nutmeg trees, fare much better.

In 1859, a new Agri-Horticultural Society was formed and acquired a 24-hectare site in the Tanglin District from a wealthy trader named Hoo Ah Kay, better known as "Whampoa", who was not only a prominent businessman but also a keen gardener. This time there was no talk of science and commerce; the purpose was simply to create a pleasure park where members of the Society could

← A Rain Tree spreads its branches over the driveway leading to the Visitor's Centre; on the right is a stand of Sealing Wax Palms (*Cyrtostachys renda*). Characterized by its bright scarlet leaf sheaths, the palm is indigenous.

→ A stand of *Vanda Miss Joaquim* orchids. Found by Miss Agnes Joaquim at the end of the 19th century in her garden, this mauve-and-white orchid was designated Singapore's National Flower in 1981. When Miss Joaquim, the daughter of a prominent Armenian family, took the specimen to Henry Nicholas Ridley, then Director of the Botanic Gardens, he confirmed that it was indeed new, a natural hybrid between *Vanda hookerana* and *V. teres*, and announced the fact in the 'Gardener's Chronicle' of 24 June 1893. *Vanda Miss Joaquim*, as it was christened, was not only beautiful but also hardy and free-flowering; it can now be found in numerous varieties.

← ← View of the Gardens' second lake, studded with three islands; known as Symphony Lake, open-air Jazz in the Park and classical concerts are often held on the stage in the lake's centre.

← The Bandstand, one of the original structures built in the Gardens for concerts; the trees are a yellow-leafed variety of the Monkeypod or Rain tree, (*Samanea saman*).

↓ Turn-of-the-century photogravure by German photographer Charles J Kleingrothe showing a view of the Gardens' first lake and the sweeping path that goes around it. Photograph courtesy of Antiques of the Orient.

enjoy themselves amid colorful flower beds that reminded them of home. Lawrence Niven, a local Nutmeg planter, laid out the original landscape, which remains more or less unchanged today. A bandstand for concerts stood on top of a terraced hill, along with a series of roads connected by pathways; by 1866, the first of three scenic lakes had been excavated on an additional strip of land along the present Tyersall Road.

The Society worked hard to fulfil its ambitions and attract visitors. Beds of brightly-colored ornamentals were planted on the terraces, a regimental band performed in the airy Victorian bandstand, and lady members organized frequent "horticultural fetes and fancy fairs"; a small zoo was added, displaying a leopard presented by the King of Siam and kangaroos from Australia; the garden was even expanded by the purchase of 10 more hectares. But despite such efforts the Society's debts grew and membership declined; in 1875, it admitted defeat and handed over maintenance to the government. The need for a qualified superintendent was clear to the new committee, and in search of one they wrote to the Royal Gardens at Kew, whose director, Sir Joseph Hooker, recommended a young botanist named Henry James Murton.

Murton's stay was relatively short – only five years – but it marked the beginning of the Botanic Gardens as a center of scientific research as well as a place for recreation. His attitude toward the carefree ways of the past was clear in his early annual reports. "It is my unpleasant duty," he wrote in one, "to report many serious infringements of the Rules, not only by natives but also by Europeans. The latter on more than one occasion have been detected cutting flowers by moonlight." He put a stop to such practices, set up exchange programs with other gardens around the world, established a library, and finally started an Economic Garden on a 41-hectare site north of the Gardens, where new commercial crops could be tested.

It was Murton who received from Kew the first seedlings of Para rubber; in 1879, the year before he left, he reported his concern over their slow rate of propagation, a problem that would be solved with dramatic results by a subsequent director (see pages 98–101).

Nathaniel Cantley, also Kew-trained, took over in 1880 and was responsible for a number of improvements, both in the administration of the gardens and in Singapore. He intitiated the town's formal tree planting, which included a "People's Park" containing more than 1000 trees and shrubs in the Chinese area.

Thereafter, the Botanic Gardens was fortunate in having a series of outstanding directors. Probably the most famous was Henry Nicholas Ridley, who followed Cantley and became known as "the father of the Malayan rubber industry" when he devised effective ways of propagating and tapping the small forest of *Hevea brasiliensis* that had been growing

← ← An Oil Palm (*Elaesis guineensis*), one of many formally planted at the new entrance area to the Gardens. Small water features with *Phoenix roebelenii* are interspersed amongst the palms in this attractive court.

← Trunks of *Cyrtostachys renda*; a row of these colorful palms lines the roadway at the entrance.

↙ A water feature just past the new entrance court; in the background can be seen the roof of Burkill Hall, once the Director's residence. The trees are Dillenias and Ficus.

ever since Murton's time. His protean energies found other outlets as well. He introduced many new commercial plants, among them the oil palm which became Malaya's second most important crop, helped explore and conserve the forests of the peninsula, expanded the Herbarium and library of rare books, and wrote several standard botanical works; it was to Ridley that Miss Agnes Joaquim came with a discovery one morning – a new natural orchid hybrid she had discovered in her garden, which in turn became Singapore's national flower. By 1955, when he celebrated his 100th birthday, he had won every possible award in his field and the event was celebrated in both Singapore and England.

Eric Holttum, another giant, is remembered for his pioneering work in orchid hybridization and culture, for founding both the Orchid Society and the Singapore Gardening Society, and for introducing numerous new ornamental plants that added to the beauty of the gardens. During the harsh years of the Japanese Occupation, he and his assistant EJH Corner were allowed to remain in the gardens and thus preserved the Herbarium and library (see pages 102–103). He became the University of Malaya's first Professor of Botany in 1949 and his seminal *Gardening in the Lowlands of Malaya* (1953) remains a standard handbook.

The Botanic Gardens faced new challenges and responsibilities in the postwar years as Singapore achieved independence. It played a major part in the campaign to beautify Singapore, first launched in 1963 by Prime Minister Lee Kuan Yew and accelerated under the "Garden City" campaign four years later. This changing mission was reflected in 1973 with the decision to merge the Gardens with Parks and Trees Branch of the Public Works Department to form the Parks and Recreations Division, raised three years later to the status of a Department; in 1990 the National Parks Board was formed and the original role and functions of the Gardens were restored.

Meanwhile the Botanic Gardens has continued its work as a center of scientific research, education, and preservation Today, it covers an area of 52 hectares (about 128 acres) in four different zones and is visited by two and a half million people a year. Its School of Ornamental Horticulture, initially founded in 1972 to train personnel for the Garden City concept, now offers courses in both tropical horticulture and landscape design. There is a Plant Introduction unit and new tropical plants are still tested in its nurseries and, if they adapt to local conditions, are released for use in Singapore's parks and along its roads.

It has also continued to attract non-specialists who merely want to stroll along the pathways and enjoy the thousands of tropical ornamentals on show. Among the most spectacular newer attractions is the National Orchid Garden (see pages 88–93), Eco Lake, a natural habitat for indigenous aquatic plants and wildlife, as well as a performance shell on Symphony Lake, a Cloud Forest Greenhouse, an air-conditioned facility that houses such temperate species as rhododendrons and high-altitude orchids, and a section devoted entirely to the Gardens' large *penjing* collection (see pages 86–87).

↓ Old postcard showing the gardens when under the auspices of the Agri-Horticultural Society. Cows were invited in to graze in the grounds!

→ Palm Valley, home to a variety of palms, among them the lofty Talipot (*Corypha umbraculifera*) and the unusual Double Coconut (*Lodoicea maldivica*) which produces the largest seed of any plant in the world. This specimen is the only male tree in the Gardens.

Singapore. Botanical Garden.

← Various species of Cycas, one of the earth's oldest plants, in the Sun Rockery.

↑ *Phoenix coureirii*, a single-trunk palm with feathery leaves.

↗ *Pereskia aculeata*, a spiny-stemmed member of the Cactus family from tropical America.

→ Various species of Agave, popularly known as the Century Plant.

→ → *Nolina recurvata*, a drought-loving member of the Liliaceae family popularly called the Pony-tail palm.

→ Fruit of *Wodyetia bifurca*, the Foxtail palm.
→ → *Elaeis guineensis*, the Oil palm, a native of Africa but now an important plantation palm.
↓ *Pigafetta filaris*, a spiny palm from Indonesia.
↘ Botanical drawing showing the Betel Nut palm (*Areca catechu*) and its popular fruit.
→ → → Leaves of *Arenga undulatifolia*.
→ → → → The Talipot palm, (*Corypha umbraculifera*) with inflorescence.
↘ ↘ → Fruit of *Phoenix roebelenii*, the Pygmy Date palm.
↘ ↘ ↘ Fruit of *Lodoicea maldivica*, or Coco-de-mer.
↘ ↘ ↘ Two-lobed nut of *Lodoicea maldivica*.
↘ ↘ ↘ ↘ *Johannesteijamannia altifrons*, a Malaysian native.

The Botanic Gardens Penjing Display

The oldest evidence of *penjing* in China was discovered in the tomb of a Tang dynasty prince in 1972 in Shaanxi Province. Dating from 706 AD, paintings on the wall show two servants, one of whom is carrying a miniature landscape composed of rocks and plants. Chinese *penjing* are divided into two kinds – those in which landscapes are created through rocks, water, and sometimes plants, known as Shan Shui Penjing, and those that are simply an artfully trained plant in a pot, known as She Zhuang Penjing. Both types developed into a number of different schools, some involving careful pruning and others in which wires are used for training the plants into particular shapes. While such creations are most often associated with temperate plants, many are also grown in the tropics as the display at the Botanic Gardens reveals. This has recently been installed on the site of the old Rose Garden, and showcases the huge number of *penjing* trees and shrubs that have been collected at the Gardens over the years.

← *Juniperus chinensis* in an octagonal decorated pot developed in the cascade style. All the *penjing* are put on shelves beneath an awning for protection. In the background are some of the flowering shrubs that surround the display area.

↖ A Ficus in upright style displaying aerial roots.

↑↑ Mrs Quek-Phua Lek Kheng of the Botanic Gardens and consultant Mr Lim Keow Wah tend to some of the specimens on display.

↑ A group planting of *Wrightia religiosa* display aerial roots and contorted shapes. *Penjing* are often arranged in groups of three.

The National Orchid Garden

Orchids comprise one of the largest and most diverse families of flowering plants, with over 25,000 species – 179 of which are native to the island of Singapore – and have been part of the Botanic Gardens' allure since the earliest days. In the 1870s, Henry Murton began cultivating species in an orchid house, and this continued under subsequent directors. RE Holttum, in charge of the Gardens from 1925 to 1949, was particularly keen on introducing new species and hybrids; it was under his leadership that several of Singapore's best-known hybrids appeared on the cut-flower market, among them *Oncidium* 'Goldiana' (a cross between *O. sphacelatum* and *O. flexuosum*), popularly known as the Golden Shower or Dancing Lady orchid, which was produced in 1939 and is now exported throughout the world.

Plans for a new and far more ambitious facility began in the 1980s, spearheaded by Dr Tan Wee Kiat, and finally achieved success in November 1995 when the National Orchid Garden was opened by Senior Minister Lee Kuan Yew. Located on the highest hill in the Gardens, it covers three hectares of naturally landscaped, gently sloping hillside.

← A pool with cascades and sculptures at the entrance to the Orchid Gardens; Bird's Nest Ferns and other epiphytes grow on the tree at right.

↗ *Arantera* 'Alice Ng', one of the many hybrids produced at the Gardens.

→ A display of Vanda hybrids in delicate pink tones grace the Enclosure.

→ *Oncidium* 'Goldiana', known as the Golden Shower or Dancing Lady orchid, one of the most popular hybrids ever produced at the Gardens. In April 1940, *The Malayan Orchid Review* described it thus: "This hybrid gives promise of being extremely free flowering under Singapore conditions and combines the bright colour of one parent with the size of the other. Though it is not a striking novelty, it is yet likely to be a most useful plant, both for pot displays and for cut flowers."

← The National Orchid Garden is divided into four zones: The spring zone features orchids in the cream, yellow and gold spectrum, summer has orchids in strong red and pink tones, autumn features more matured shades, while winter consists entirely of white orchids. Palms and ground orchids add to the lush, jungle atmosphere.

↖ *Oncidium sarcutum*.

↑ Orchids on display, together with a number of ornamentals notable for their distinctive leaf patterns.

← Archway in the Orchid Garden, planted with *Oncidium* 'Goldiana'.

→ Various hybrid Phalaenopsis, popularly called the Moth Orchid.

↓ A hybrid Paphiopedilum, one of the Lady Slipper Orchids, so named because of the pouch-like lip that resembles a lady's slipper.

↘ *Phalaenopsis bellum*, formerly known as *P. violacea* Witte, a species with a sweet fragrance from Borneo.

There are regular displays of more than 700 orchid species (mainly acquired through collection trips, exchange programmes and donations) and 2,100 hybrids (many bred at the Gardens themselves), as well as numerous other exotic tropical plants. Of the many genera in the collection, Dendrobium is the largest, followed by such vandaceous species as Arachnis, Vanda, Renanthera, and Phalaenopsis, though Bulbophyllum, Papiopedilum, and Oncidium are also well represented. Perhaps the most popular exhibit is the VIP Orchid Garden, containing hybrids named after various dignitaries, a practice that began in the Gardens nearly three decades ago.

In addition to a changing display of flowering orchids on trees and in hanging pots, the Enclosure also features the Tan Hoon Siang Mist House, where the humid atmosphere of a rain forest is reproduced, and the Yuen-Peng McNeice Bromeliad Collection, which was acquired in Florida and donated to the Gardens by one of its most loyal supporters. An elegant 1866 structure that served as the residence of past Directors, has been preserved as a center for refreshments and displays.

↖ *Erythrina crista-galli*, one of the numerous flowering trees that are planted alongside the orchids as anchors in the Enclosure.

← A worker in the Orchid Gardens; staff are constantly in attendance tending, watering and generally overseeing the status of the plants in the Enclosure.

Orchid Research and Propagation

Scientific cultivation of orchids began at the Singapore Botanic Gardens during Eric Holttum's term as Director (1925–49). During a visit in the late '20s, Professor Hans Burgeff of Wutrzburg introduced Holttum to the method developed by the American Lewis Knudson, in which seeds were grown in sterile culture media, and by 1929 he had used it to germinate numerous seedlings at the Gardens; his first successful hybrid, in 1931, was a cross between *Spathoglottis aurea* and *Spathoglottis plicata*, called *S.* 'Primrose'. This and others developed during his time, such as the famous *Oncidium* 'Goldiana' (Golden Shower), became the basis of Singapore's cut-flower industry. New hybrids have appeared regularly at the Gardens ever since. *Vanda* 'Tan Chay Yan', named after the first successful rubber grower, first flowered in 1952 and

↑ → Laboratory at the Botanic Gardens where orchid seedlings are cultivated in sterile culture media, a method first introduced to the Gardens by Eric Holttum in the 1920s. The Breeding programme proceeds apace: Between 1990 and 1994, 40 hybrids were registered; one of these was a new hybrid – *Vanda* Singa Joaquim Centenary – bred to commemorate the 100th birthday of *Vanda* Miss Joaquim, Singapore's National Flower. It is the progeny of a cross between *Vanda* Josephine van Brero and *Vanda* Miss Joaquim.

went on to win a First Class Certificate at the Chelsea Flower show in London. In the early 1980s, under the direction of Dr Tan Wee Kiat, the Gardens produced hundreds of new hybrids for display in the Gardens and for local commercial orchid growers.

Tissue culture, pioneered by GM Moret of France, came to the Gardens in 1960, and a tissue culture laboratory was established in the early 1970s. This proved a great success in mass propagation of orchid species and hybrids, 624 of which had been produced by the end of 1998. Today, research is centered on molecular diagnostics for quality control of tissue cultured orchids and more efficient non-destructive tissue culture techniques. In breeding, stress will be placed on new colors and longer-lasting hybrids, while in the area of orchid conservation, species population will be increased through seeding culture, dissemination to other botanical institutions and re-introduction into their natural habitats.

Famous Singapore Hybrid Orchids

Of the numerous orchid hybrids introduced at the Gardens, many are named after famous people, institutions and organizations. The first, in 1956, was *Aranthera* 'Anne Black', named after the wife of Sir Robert Black, a former Governor of Singapore. Since then, such visiting dignitaries as Indira Ghandi, Margaret Thatcher, Nelson Mandela, Emperor Akihito of Japan and Queen Elizabeth II have been similarly honored, as well as the less well-known Jane Denny, who received her orchid when she became Singapore's four millionth visitor. Local dignitaries have been similarly honoured: the wife of the first President of Singapore has the orchid *Dendrobium* 'Noor Aishah', while the wife of Senior Minister Lee Kuan Yew was presented with her hybrid *Ascosenda* 'Kwa Geok Choo' on the occasion of the opening of the National Orchid Garden.

↙ Massed displays just outside the entrance to the National Orchid Garden.

↙ *Renanthera* Akihito (*Renanthera* Red Feathers x *Renanthera storiei*), named after the Emperor Akihito of Japan.

→ *Dendrobium* Memoria Princess Diana (*Dendrobium* Pattaya Beauty x *Dendrobium* Fairy Wong); this orchid was named in memory of Princess Diana on September 22, 1997.

→ → *Dendrobium* Singapore Girl Orchid (*Dendrobium* Singa Rose x *Dendrobium* Alkaff Melisa White), named on June 12, 1997 to commemorate the 50th anniversary of Singapore Airlines.

↘ *Dendrobium* Margaret Thatcher (*Dendrobium* Concham x *Dendrobium* lasianthera), named after the UK's former prime minister, Baroness Thatcher, during her visit to the gardens in 1985).

↘ ↘ *Dendrobium* Elizabeth (*Dendrobium* Mustard x *Dendrobium* Noor Aishah), named after Queen Elizabeth 11 of the UK during her visit to the Botanic Gardens in 1972.

Other hybrids include *Dendrobium* 'World Peace', *D.* 'Rotary International', *Mokara* 'World Trade Organization' and *Vanda* 'Overseas Union Bank', to name a few.

The Story of Rubber

Both in Palm Valley and near the Herbarium in the Botanic Gardens there grow a number of Para rubber trees, *Hevea brasiliensis*, a reminder of the crucial role played by the Gardens in the development of this important commercial crop.

Popular legend has it that the first rubber tree seeds were smuggled out of Brazil by one Henry Wickham, an intrepid British botanist. In fact, around 70,000 were collected with the approval of the Brazilian authorities in 1876 and sent to Kew where, depressingly, only some three percent were successfully germinated. Of 22 seedlings sent to Singapore the following year, half went to various places in Malaya and just 11 were planted in the Botanic Gardens by Henry Murton.

There they languished for more than 10 years, suffering from a slow rate of propagation and also from a lack of interest among Malayan planters, who were mainly committed to coffee at the time.

← A grove of Para rubber trees (*Hevea brasiliensis*) in the Botanic Gardens, near the present Herbarium. A memorial marker to Nicholas Ridley is placed at the site of the original planting of rubber trees in Palm Valley.

→ Rubber latex dripping from a tree into a pot.

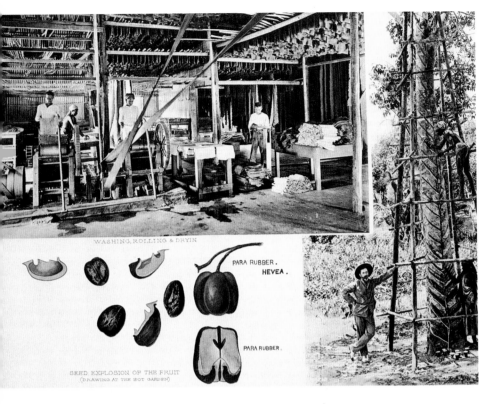

WASHING, ROLLING & DRYIN

PARA RUBBER.
HEVEA.

PARA RUBBER.

SEED EXPLOSION OF THE FRUIT
(DRAWING AT THE BOT GARDEN)

Only when Henry Nicholas Ridley became Director in 1888 was real progress made on the tiny grove of trees. Ridley not only devised speedier ways of propagation but, even more important, a method of tapping the latex without killing the tree. Despite official disapproval, he became so obsessed with the idea of rubber as a viable crop that he became known as 'Mad Ridley', ceaselessly travelling around Malaya with seeds in an effort to encourage planters to try some.

Several developments finally led to success. Tan Chay Yan, a tapioca planter in Malacca, agreed to devote 16 hectares to rubber in 1896 with seeds supplied by Ridley. A few years later the coffee market collapsed (caused, ironically, by an over-supply from Brazil) and, almost simultaneously, there was a worldwide demand for bicycle and automobile tires. Planters then got the message: from 400 tons in 1905, rubber production soared to over 210,000 tons in 1920 and Malaya had a major new industry that still flourishes today.

↑ Old photographs by CJ Kleingrothe showing aspects of the rubber industry: the seeds and fruits of the tree, a tree with cross-hatch cuts to tap the latex, and the process of washing, rolling, and drying the latex sheets. Photo courtesy of Antiques of the Orient.

→ Rubber plantations used to stretch from the southernmost tip of Peninsular Malaysia up into Thailand, but many have now been replaced with Oil Palm plantations.

→ → *Hevea brasiliensis* specimens in the Herbarium, collected in 1921.

The Herbarium and Library

Among the greatest treasures of the Botanic Gardens is the Herbarium, which relatively few outsiders ever see. Here, meticulously filed in cabinets is a collection of over 600,000 dried and preserved botanical specimens gathered on numerous expeditions, a priceless resource that started under Henry James Murton, the Gardens' first Kew-trained Superintendent. It was formally established in 1880 under Nathaniel Cantley, the Superintendent of the Gardens from 1880–88, and now benefits not only local researchers but others all over the world.

Fruits, leaves, and flowers in the collection are dried, chemically treated, and identified before being filed away. New specimens are constantly being added, while duplicates are exchanged with other herbaria. In addition, the Gardens also has a collection of over 20,000 books on botany and horticulture, many of them rare editions, as well as some 500 current journals. It is the best library of its kind in Asia.

↖ The gifted botanist EJH Corner, Assistant Director of the Gardens from 1929–45, with two or his berok or pig-tailed monkeys (*Macacus nemestrina*). With the help of a Malay trainer, he instructed the monkeys to retrieve plant material from tree tops by pointing out similar specimens on the ground.

← Haji Mohammed Shah, a researcher at the Herbarium looks through some of the more than half a million dried botanic specimens stored in the Herbarium. Haji Mohammed Shah has worked at the Botanic Gardens for over 40 years.

Filed in cabinets in the Herbarium lie thousands of dried specimens of flowers, leaves and fruits, along with notes as to where they were collected, who collected them, the date and any relevant information. A selection are photographed here:

→ *Nepenthes rafflesiana*, collected by HN Ridley on Mt Ophir in June, 1892.

→ → *Rafflesia Hasseltii* Sur., collected on June 11, 1937.

↘ *Entada schefferi*, collected in 1988 in Johore, Malaysia.

↘ ↘ *Nepenthes villosa* Hook f., collected by CE Carr in Kanborangah-Pakka on June 8, 1933.

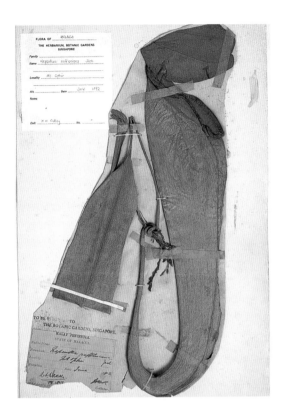

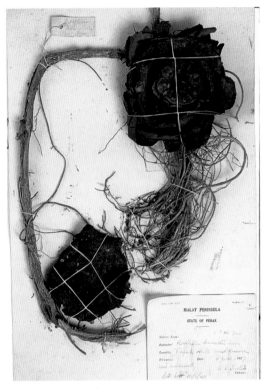

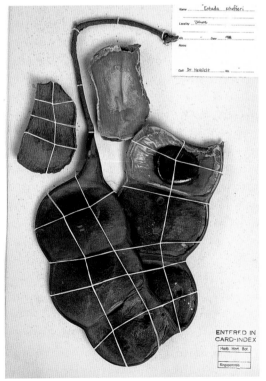

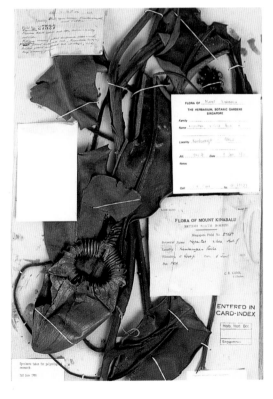

Exotic Vines

Displayed on trellises, gazebos, and other supports in various parts of the Gardens are many of the colorful flowering creepers for which the tropics is famous. Among the most spectacular is the Jade Vine (*Strongylodon macrobotrys*) a native of the Philippine jungle which has hanging clusters of extraordinary blue-green flowers, a memorable sight when the vine is in full bloom. Also of the same botanical family, Leguminosae, is the New Guinea Creeper (*Mucuna bennettii*), with similar flowers that are a vivid red-orange; this vine was introduced to the Gardens by way of seeds collected in the New Guinea jungles in 1940. Elsewhere can be seen *Odontadenia macrantha*, producing fragrant tubular apricot flowers almost year-round; the Garlic Vine (*Mansoa alliacea*) which releases a strong garlic scent when the plant is bruised; white-flowering *Beaumontia multiflora*; and the Honolulu Creeper (*Antigonon leptopus*).

← ← *Mansoa alliacea (Pseudocalmma alliaceum)*, the Garlic Vine, in full bloom across a support.

← *Odontadenia macrantha*, a delicate-looking bloom.

↙ *Mucuna bennettii*, the New Guinea Creeper; this came into prominence after a Flower Show in the late 1940s.

↓ *Strongydodon macrobotrys*, the Jade Vine.

Mount Faber Park

Offering panoramic views of the sea and southern off-shore islands, Mount Faber Park is one of the oldest in Singapore and has long been a popular place for recreation. A tree was added to the highest point on the first "Tree Planting Day" in 1971, a symbolic milestone in the "greening" campaign, and the park was recently redeveloped with new plantings, lookout points toward various regional capitals from the ridge, a series of pathways and rest areas, and a collection of bas-reliefs showing notable events in Singapore's history.

Secondary rain forest covers much of Mount Faber, along with such decorative specimens as Alstonia, the Red Flame tree (*Delonix regia*), the Rain tree (*Samanea saman*), the Golden Shower (*Cassia fistula*), Fir (*Pinus eliotii*) and Bougainvillea. A station for cable cars going to the adjacent island of Sentosa is also located in the park.

← A rain tree (*Samanea saman*) was planted at the top of Mount Faber when the park was redesigned, while Bougainvillea grows in containers on either side.

↑ View of Sentosa island, accessible by cable car; the red flowering shrub is Ixora.

→ The merlion, symbol of Singapore, is surrounded by low-growing *Arachis pintoi*, a member of the peanut family.

→ → The skyscrapers of part of the city can be seen from the summit of Mount Faber; the white flowers on the right are Hymenocallis, planted along pathways in the park.

Sentosa Island

Located just off Singapore's southern coast, Sentosa has a varied history. Once known as Blakang Mati, "Behind Death", it was a military center in the pre-war days of British rule with a fortress designed to protect Singapore from invasion by sea. The huge guns proved useless when the enemy arrived down by way of the Malayan peninsula; instead the island became a notorious camp for British, Australian and Indian prisoners of war. In the late 1980s, its name was changed to Sentosa – a Malay word meaning "peace" or "tranquillity" – and an enormous sum was spent transforming the island into a vast theme park that now attracts millions of visitors annually.

Accessible by bridge or cable car – a spectacular ride from either Mount Faber Park or the World Trade Center – Sentosa offers a variety of attractions set in a well-tended landscape of tropical beauty. A highlight is the towering merlion, a mythological half-lion, half-fish creature that acts as Singapore's official mascot. Other popular features include a musical fountain with both day and nighttime shows, model Asian villages, a series of historical images that range from the arrival of Raffles to the city's surrender in 1942, a huge aquarium, three white-sand beaches, and a nature walk that leads through secondary rainforest to the top of a hill.

← The island of Sentosa as seen from the cablecar.

↗ One of three beaches, lined with coconut palms.

↗ Barracks built in the days when Sentosa was a British military stronghold.

→ The merlion, official mascot of Singapore; elevators inside carry visitors up for panoramic views over to Singapore. In front is the formal planting known as the Flower Walk.

← A colourful mosaic sculpture designed by landscape architect Henry Steed depicting various creatures from the sea.

↑ A monorail carries visitors on a tour of Sentosa's attractions, including the merlion.

↗↗ Spice and Herb garden, planted with the very trees and shrubs of the Indo-Malay Archipelago that first lured Europeans to the Far East. Opposite is the Scented Garden, which has such specimens as Jasmine, Honeysuckle, Cananga and Champaka.

→ An overview of the entire island, looking towards Sentosa across a harbor where ocean liners dock.

← ↙ Palms in plastic containers stand in the nursery prior to being moved to one of Singapore's parks. Those seen at the top are *Bismarkia nobilis*, while those at the bottom are used in avenues.

→ Thousands of Cordylines and other ornamental plants are maintained in the nursery for future use in public landscapes.

↘ Workers move a small tree, destined to be planted along one of Singapore's streets as "instant trees".

Pasir Panjang Nursery

Established in the 1970s to supply the needs of Singapore's parks, playgrounds, and roadsides, the Pasir Panjang nursery maintains a broad range of trees and shrubs, an average of some 400,000 at any given time. Over half a million were issued by the nursery in 1998 alone, an increase of 40 per cent over the previous year.

The nursery itself is huge, covering an area of 20 hectares, and large parts of it are serviced by a fully-automated watering system. Plants in the nursery are selected both for attractive appearance and proven ability to grow well in Singapore's environment and climate. Many are long-standing favorites like the Yellow Flame (*Peltophorum pterocarpum*), the Rain tree (*Samanea saman*), and the African Mahogany (*Khaya senegalensis*), while others have been introduced more recently through the Botanic Gardens' Plant Introduction Unit.

Wayside Trees

Of all the trees that shade Singapore's streets, the most common in the early days was the Angsana (*Pterocarpus indicus*). A fast-growing species native to the Malay Peninsula, Angsanas were planted in Malacca in the 18th century and later used extensively along boulevards in both Penang and Singapore. A disease that began in Malacca in 1885 and reached to Singapore in 1914 wiped out most of the older trees, though many new ones were planted at the beginning of the Garden City campaign, often as "instant trees" produced from large cuttings. Other long-standing favorites include the umbrella-shaped Rain tree (*Samanea saman*), the Yellow Flame (*Peltophorum pterocarpum*), the False Mahogany (*Swietenia macrophylla*) and the Red Flame (*Delonix regia*). No longer planted so often are the African Tulip (*Spathodea campanulata*), a fast-grower but easily felled by strong winds; many varieties of Ficus with their invasive roots; and the Kapok (*Ceiba pentandra*), the fibre-filled pods of which create a maintenance problem.

New wayside trees are constantly being introduced, especially in recent years. A Yellow Rain tree, genetically different from the ordinary species, has proved useful for foliage contrast in a wet climate not favorable for most flowering trees, as has the Wild Cinnamon (*Cinnamomum iners*) on which the new leaves are bright red. Palms are also popular, among them *Caryota bradiata*, a variety of Fishtail palm which was introduced from Sarawak, and is now widely used along entrances and exits to tunnels and expressways.

← Rain Trees (*Samanea saman*) planted along both sides of a residential street form a canopy as they join overhead. Brought to Singapore around 1876 from South America, they are a popular wayside tree, particularly as their corky bark provides a suitable medium for ephiphytic plants such as *Asplenium nidus*, other ferns, and a variety of orchids (the Pigeon orchid being but one example).

← Planted traditionally in residential streets, the native *Cerbera odollam* or Pong-pong tree is now being uprooted because buried within the fruits is a single poisonous seed.

→ *Filicium decipiens*, the Fern Tree, was introduced from Sri Lanka or south India around 1875 into the Botanic Gardens. Rows of this tree may be seen in many residential streets and also in front of Tanglin Shopping Centre.

→ → *Tabebuia pallida*, or the Tecoma tree, is seen along Upper Paya Lebar Road, amongst others.

↘ The Yellow Flame tree (*Peltophorum pterocarpum*) came from the coastal areas of the Malay Peninsula.

↘ ↘ The Cannon Ball tree from South America is strange looking, as its fruit and flowers grow simultaneously from the trunk. It may be seen on Tanglin Road and Cross Street.

↘ The Plumeria is everyone's favorite; this deep pink flowering variety is planted at the intersection of Paterson and Grange Roads, and seems to be permanently in flower.

↘ ↘ The *Lagerstroemia* sp (Pride of India) all burst into flower simultaneously over the island, bringing a mass of lilac, lavender and pink to the city.

← Planted frequently in the middle of roads, the colourful *Cassia fistula* or Golden Shower tree has beautiful, pendant blooms.

The Chinese Garden

Operated by the Jurong Town Corporation, the Chinese Garden (Yu Hwa Yuan) was opened in 1975 as part of a larger recreational development project that also includes the nearby Japanese Garden and the famous Jurong Bird Park. It covers approximately 13 hectares and is modelled on the classical style of imperial gardens that flourished during the Sung Dynasty. Recently refurbished, the garden provides a broad introduction to traditional Chinese architecture and landscaping. Among the features that can be seen around a picturesque lake beyond the colourfully-tiled entrance gate are an elegant nine-tiered pagoda, airy tea pavilions, moon gates, and arched red bridges, as well as reproductions of buildings in Beijing's Summer Palace. A Garden of Fragrance, planted with scented specimens, is a popular spot for young married couples to be photographed beside stone plaques carved with auspicious signs, while a Herb Garden contains plants used in Chinese medicines. There is also a representative collection of Bamboo, a plant that plays a significant role in Chinese art and daily life.

Special events are held on such occasions as the Lantern Festival in the eighth Lunar month, but for the most part, the Chinese Garden offers the opportunity for a tranquil stroll in peaceful and not-too-crowded surroundings.

← A romantic tea pavilion in a shady grove overlooks a winding river.

↗ Reproductions of classic Chinese palace buildings are reflected in the lake; in the foreground is a yellow Bamboo.

→ The nine-tiered pagoda forms part of a traditional setting in an industrialized area of the city.

The Suzhou Penjing Garden

Two 300-year-old Podocarpus trees from China clipped in the form of lions flank the entrance to the Suzhou Penjing Garden, a series of walled courtyards in which are displayed examples of *penjing*, a skill that goes back thousands of years. This garden within a garden was opened in 1992 by Dr Goh Keng Swee and attracts not only fanciers of the ancient art of growing miniature potted plants but also others interested in a variety of Chinese landscape features.

Penjing is a specialist Oriental horticulture art that originated in China during the Tang Dynasty. There are five main schools of *penjing*, namely the Guangdong style, the Sichuan style, the Yangzhou style, the Suzhou/Hangzhou style and the Shanghai style; examples of all five may be found within the Yun Xiu Yuan as the garden is known. With over

Previous page (right): One of the courtyards in the Suzhou Penjing Garden, a 1992 addition to the Chinese Garden; examples of *penjing*, are displayed on stands along a pebbled pathway with a "moon gate" at the end.

Previous page (left): An unusual gateway in the shape of a vase leads from one courtyard to the another. Note the change of texture in the mosaic pathway and the example of Chinese calligraphy above the arch.

2000 *penjing* from China, Taiwan, Japan, Malaysia, Indonesia, Thailand and the Philippines as well as from Singapore, the garden also has a collection of rockery *penjing* from Jingjiang in Jiangsu Province.

Designed by a renowned architect from Suzhou and constructed by Suzhou craftsmen, each walled courtyard is designed to flow into the next. There are four main areas, comprising the miniature *penjing* area, the tree *penjing* area, the masterpiece *penjing* area and the rockery *penjing* area. At every turn there is something new to explore, be it a view through an archway or "moon gate" to a different vista; a small room containing a collection of "artistic Stones"; Chinese characters depicting various good-luck motifs; pebbled mosaic pathways; stones collected at Lake Tai in Suzhou Provinces, or windows that frame a particularly evocative view.

← ← The entrance courtyard has a whitewashed display stand with miniature *penjing* and a large abstract stone sculpture. Such rocks are not carved, but simply collected and displayed if they have a particularly pleasing shape. In the foreground is a shiny-leved, clipped Podocarpus.

↑ Pathways display a variety of decorative forms; there are a number of classic buildings as well.

← *Wrightia religiosa* specimen with trunk trained to grow into the shape of a unique Chinese "good-luck" character.

← A small courtyard with a single *penjing* specimen flanked by two rocks may be viewed from a number of different "windows". Each is framed in a different pattern.

↙ ↓ In the final courtyard one area is devoted to the display of a collection of "tray landscapes".

→ An overview of the Rockery Courtyard, where tropical green sets off such features as a graceful pavilion and an arched bridge. In addition to the *penjing*, there are a number of other shrubs and plants, including *Musa* sp and Bamboo.

Chinese Traditions

While Singapore prides itself on its multi-racial character, Chinese traditions unquestionably predominate. Chinese temples with their curving tiled roofs and ornate decorations can be seen all over the city, and so can the various festivals and emblems that mark the culture. During the seventh Lunar month, for example, the so-called Hungry Ghosts Festival is held, during which many Chinese appease disturbed spirits with an offering of food and burning joss paper. The colourful Lantern Festival, in turn, is observed on the fifteenth day of the eighth Lunar month; lighted paper and plastic lanterns glow along city streets, and at a special celebration held in the Chinese Garden. The biggest festival of all, of course, is Chinese New Year, another Lunar event that falls in January or February, which a major part of the population celebrates by decorating houses, paying respect to elders, and giving and receiving red gift packets containing money for good luck.

Plants figure prominently in Chinese traditions. Orange represents gold or wealth and red suggests good fortune, and any plants that display those colours in flowers or leaves are regarded as promoting prosperity; yellow, pink, and pinky-purple flowers are also favored. Pots of miniature orange trees (a form of Calamondin) are placed outside homes and shops. *Celosia cristata*, with pyramidal masses of tiny red or yellow flowers is also a popular good-luck plant, as are roses, pink Dendrobium orchids, and cut stems of Pussy Willow (Salix) buds. Growing in many traditional Chinese gardens all year round are *Aglaia odorata*, a shrub with tiny scented flowers, and *Platycladus orientalis*, a kind of cypress, both of which are deemed to be auspicious.

↖ The Lantern Festival, in the eighth Lunar month, is a major celebration in the Chinese Garden.

← A Chinese temple amid modern buildings; a Rain tree grows on the right.

↑ → Decorations and gifts for Chinese New Year – miniature orange trees and *Celosia cristata* in "golden" colors. Because of the tropical climate, traditional Chinese spring flowers such as Plum Blossom, Pussy Willow and sweet-scented Narcissus have to be imported. Due to the cost, many Singaporean Chinese substitute with pink and light purple Dendrobiums and other orchids in order to achieve a similar color and effect.

A Private Penjing Collection

The artfully trained plants shown on these pages are part of the collection of Mr Lim Keow Wah, of the Singapore Penjing and Stone Appreciation Society. Displayed on raised stands at the front of his city home, Mr Lim uses many different species for his creations. Among them are *Juniperus chinensis*, which has small, green or blue-green needle-like leaves and occurs in both prostrate and conical forms; *Wrightia religiosa*, a fast-growing shrub with fragrant white flowers; and Caelsapinia, with bright red or yellow flowers. A 200-year-old *Pemphis acidula* with a driftwood trunk grows on coral and must only be given salt water. While most of the species are tropical or sub-tropical they are trained to look like the classical temperate trees of Chinese *penjing* or Japanese *bonsai*. Regular clipping and wire training ensure they keep their various shapes.

← ← ← A Juniperus in the twisted trunk style known as *ban kan*.

↑ *Baeckea frutescens* in the semi-cascade style is distinguished by its driftwood-type trunk.

← ← *Wrightia religiosa* in a forest tree form. A popular *penjing* plant, it has small pendant sweetly-scented flowers.

← A group of miniature *penjing* demonstrating various styles and displayed in the traditional manner. Clockwise from top are *Caesalpinia ferrea*, *Wrightia religiosa*, *Juniperus chinensis*, *Hibiscus tiliaceus* and *Wrightia religiosa*.

A Tray Landscape Collection

Mr Hoo Hai Chew lives in one of Singapore's suburban terrace houses which, from the outside, looks little different from numerous others in the city. Inside the gate, however, a magical world reveals itself. Arrayed on long shelves is a collection of tray landscapes involving both plants and stones, while built into the front courtyard is a far larger creation which evokes a complete world of rocky mountains, waterfalls, pools, houses, pagodas, and other structures.

Mr Hoo, who travels regularly to China, took up the art of miniature gardening some 30 years ago when he decided to create a replica of the Stone Forest near Kunming. This was soon followed by others until he became an acknowledged master, winning an Award of Distinction for a 124-centimetre rock landscape at the Third Asia-Pacific Bonsai and Suiseki Convention and Exhibition in 1995. Both stones and plants for Mr Hoo's collection are selected with a discerning eye for the desired aesthetic effect and then painstakingly tended. Since little soil is used, frequent watering is required to keep the roots from drying out; the plants must also be regularly pruned to maintain the delicate balance between the various elements of the arrangement.

← Examples of Mr Hoo's tray gardens, in which unusual rocks, plants and mosses suggest natural landscapes. Mr Hoo collects the natural materials for his creations from all over the world. He recalled bringing some stones back from New Zealand on one occasion.

→ The largest of the displays, set in the courtyard in front of the house. A complex world is created in this miniature landscape, similar to that found in Chinese painting.

← ← At one side of the house, Dr Chou Sip King has built a realistic-looking rocky mountain setting complete with pagodas and other buildings. A yellow orchid on the left gives an idea of the scale.

← The gigantic model at the front of the house depicting a river flowing through a Chinese village at the foot of a forested hill relies on different stone textures to set the scene.

↓ Each structure is meticulously modelled to fit into the traditional landscape.

A Chinese-style Miniature Garden

The reproduction of idealized landscapes in reduced scale is an ancient art in China. Most often it is seen in a form known as *p'an-tsai* or "table culture" (from which the Japanese word *bonsai* is derived), where a few rocks and dwarf plants are arranged in the limited confines of a single low dish (see previous page). A retired Singapore doctor, however, in search of a hobby, has created an extraordinary miniature garden that is much larger and arguably more impressive than these traditional ones.

Built in three areas of his garden, it contains literally thousands of miniature houses, pagodas and other structures in a setting that includes paths, rivers, precipitous mountain peaks and assorted plants. The result is a magical little world that recalls the scenes in classic Chinese paintings.

MacRitchie Reservoir and Park

MacRitchie Reservoir, named after a one-time Municipal Engineer, is the focal point of an unusually tranquil park that attracts joggers and other sports-minded citizens. Development of the area began in 1969 and still continues. In addition to such facilities as walking paths, excercise stations, a childrens' playground and a restaurant, it has a large number of decorative trees and shrubs, among them the handsome Yellow Flame tree (*Peltophorum pterocarpum*) and the wild Cinnamon (*Cinnamon iners*), on which the young leaves range from pink to bright red. The reservoir is one of several on the island; it is located within the central catchment area, a thickly forested, relatively untouched area. During the war, a Shinto shrine called the Syonan Jinja was built by POWs on the shore, but the Japanese destroyed it when defeat was imminent. Today, all that remains of this large structure are the 125 stone steps leading up to the shrine.

← A large Yellow Flame tree (*Peltophorum pterocarpum*) in a park-like area beside the reservoir.

↗ A pavilion providing views of the water.

→ Natural views like this are within a short drive of downtown Singapore.

The Singapore Zoological Gardens

Covering some 100 hectares at the end of Mandai Lake Road, the Singapore Zoological Gardens is one of the world's best, home to more than 2,000 animals. Situated on a spectacular promontory that is surrounded almost entirely by the waters of the Upper Seletar Reservoir, the zoo and adjacent Night Safari are one of the republic's strongest tourist attractions. Approximately 40 of the species represented, among them the Sumatran tiger, the Malayan tapir and the orangutan, are classified as endangered and have been the object of special breeding programs.

Moats rather than cages are used to separate most of the animals from their human visitors, and the spaces between have been landscaped with a variety of ornamental plants, some of them rare, to create one of the most beautiful large-scale gardens in Singapore. Of special interest is the collection of Heliconias, gingers and related plants, which thrive in the humid climate and offer an impressive display of blooms year-round (see following pages). Another notable attraction is the Fragile Forest, opened in 1998, which shows the relationship between plants, animals and humans in an enclosure where brightly-coloured butterflies flit through the carefully selected greenery and assorted small mammals can be glimpsed along the pathways. Also of interest are the lakeside formal plantings and the area devoted to fruits, vegetables, herbs and spices.

← A formal planting adjacent one shore of the reservoir is quaintly named "A Garden with a View". Dedicated to the founder of the zoo Dr Ong Swee Law, clipped hedges are lined with low flowering shrubs, including dwarf Ixora, and punctuated at intervals with Juniper trees.

↑ ↑ Another shoreside area is devoted entirely to economic crops. In the foreground are two species of ornamental pineapple.

↑ Picturesque views abound. Behind the bench and railing, are a flowering clump of *Orthosiphon aristatus*.

Heliconia Valley

One of the most striking parts of the Zoological Gardens is a walkway just inside the entrance, where a stream has been lushly planted with ornamental plants. Members of the large ginger family, some giant tree ferns, and, most of all, Heliconias provide a constant show of spectacular blooms, regularly refreshed by misty sprays that approximate their native growing conditions.

Some species of Heliconia have long been grown in Singapore, adding reliable splashes of vivid color to the predominantly green gardens. In recent years, however, numerous new species have been introduced, mostly imported from their native tropical America. Today there are an estimated 250 named varieties and almost as many forms or cultivars developed by enthusiasts. Heliconias come in a wide range of sizes, from dwarfs to giants that tower several meters. The inflorescences, actually small flowers surrounded by showy bracts, are

← ← *Heliconia chartaceae* 'Sexy Pink' and giant ferns are planted along a stream with a ground cover of red *Costus curvibracteaus* below From the 1970s on, the Mandai Orchid Gardens (see pages 142–147) were primarily responsible for the introduction into Singapore of Heliconia species.

↑ A superb example of *Heliconia vellegeria*, with a large hairy inflorescence.

← *Calathea loesenerii*, used as a ground cover in the area surrounding Heliconia Valley.

equally varied; some stand erect, while others hang down like gaudy, bright chandeliers. Several varieties are grown mainly for their decorative foliage, which may be purple, bronzy red, or delicately striped.

Among those that can be seen at the Zoological Gardens are the huge *Heliconia caribaea*, on which the bracts may be rich red, bright gold, vermillion, emerald green, or a mixture; *H. wagneriana*, with jewel-like bracts in a combination of pink, yellow, and green; *H. stricta*, in a variety of bright colors; and numerous, ever-blooming *H. psittacorum* cultivars with such descriptive names as Lady Di, Parakeet, Sassy, and Strawberries and Cream; the bright-red, hanging *H. rostrata*; a giant with broad, dense hanging bracts popularly called the Beef-steak Heliconia (*H. mariae*); and, among the most beautiful, the delicate pink variety, *H. chartacea*, known as Sexy Pink. Also planted in this area are assorted Alpinia, Costus, Calathea and Zingiber, all of which have unusual flowers.

← A display of hanging Heliconias; on the left is *Heliconia chartacea*, and in the center is *H. rostrata*. In the water may be seen the huge leaves of *Victoria amazonica*.

↑ One of the many cultivars of *Heliconia stricta*.

→ *Heliconia mariae*, the Beefsteak Heliconia.

→ → This *Heliconia pogonantha* is particularly striking with a large, pendulous cascade of alternating bracts.

Mandai Orchid Gardens

For nearly half a century, the Mandai Orchid Gardens have played an influential role, not only in the commercial cultivation of orchids for cut flowers but also, and perhaps more significantly, through its introduction of new ornamental plants and its demonstration of their dramatic landscape possibilities. The gardens were started by Lee Kim Hong and John Laycock, a lawyer, politician and keen orchid grower who, in the pre-war years, was a founder member of the Malayan Orchid Society. In 1950, they purchased five acres (later expanded to ten) in a then-remote district for an enterprise called Singapore Orchids Pte Ltd. It was taken over in 1953 by Laycock's daughter Amy and her husband John Ede, who proceeded to turn it into a highly successful venture that has developed many new hybrids and exported cut flowers worldwide.

The orchids, thousands blooming spectacularly in rows on a hillside, are still the star attraction for the busloads of tourists who come to the Mandai Gardens daily to marvel at their beauty and take pictures of such favorites as Vanda Miss Joaquim, the national flower of Singapore. (There are also

→ The Black Scorpion Orchid (*Arachnis flosaeris*), one of the more sinister-looking orchids grown at the gardens.

→ → Orchids are displayed in a blaze of changing colour at the Mandai Gardens, one of the republic's most successful tourist attractions since the 1950s. The orchids have been planted in the same way for 50 years.

← The Water Garden at the Mandai Gardens, planted with a huge clump of *Dracaena reflexa*, its colour reflected in the clump of *Crinum Xanthophyllum*, Cordylines, Heliconia and other tropical ornamentals.

→ The orchid named after Amy Ede (*Aerides* 'Amy Ede'). In her mid-70s, Amy Ede still plays an active role in the routine maintenance of the gardens. Of its beauty she says: "There can be only one reason and that is that the blessing of God is upon it." Deep religious faith has inspired and sustained her over the years, and in a useful book called *Living With Plants*, which deals with the basics of gardening in Singapore, the Edes listed some of the questions they were most commonly asked by admiring visitors. To one, "Why does everything grow so profusely and look so healthy?", there was a simple answer: "There is a lot of love in our garden".

→ Flower sprays on *Grammatohyllum speciosum*, the largest orchid in the world. Also known as the "tiger orchid" due to the markings on the flowers that resemble a tiger skin, a mature plant weighs over one ton. More than 30 flowers can be borne on the 2-m-long inflorescence. Individual flowers measure 10 cm across.

hybrids named after Amy and John Ede, their daughter and grandchildren, and, of course, John Laycock.) But for tropical gardeners the magnet is likely to be an area at the bottom of the hill that was once a marshy swamp, too wet for orchid growing and generally an eyesore.

The Edes decided to turn this area into a landscaped garden. Utilising an existing stream that never runs dry even in drought, they brought in lorry loads of soil to raise the ground level, and then planted an ever-growing collection of ornamentals in beds so placed that each turn of a pathway revealed new vistas of color and texture. The result is one of Singapore's most imaginative gardens, at once a showcase for countless varieties and a demonstration of how they can be effectively employed in a tropical landscape. Here the Edes introduced many varieties of Heliconias, Cordylines, Hibiscus, gingers, and other plants that were new to Singapore. Constantly changing and always meticulously maintained, the Water Garden, as the area is known, has been an inspiration to several generations of local and regional gardeners.

← The Water Garden with a showy display of the best foliage plants used in Singapore. Among the specimens are variegated Dracaena, Cordyline, Codiaeum, Acalypha and Graphtophyllum.

↙ A sunny lawn with many variegated plants including *Ananas comosus*, together with *Cuphea hyssopifolia* (false Heather), green-and-white Dieffenbachia and a dwarf Malvaviscus.

→ A water lily pond, part of the stream, bordered by a pink-flowering form of *Alpinia purpurata*, Hymenocallis, and Papyrus; in the background is a stand of giant Heliconia and a fine feathery Bamboo.

↑ The main lake of the Jurong Bird Park, in which an island is largely devoted to colourful Bougainvillea.

← An area between the monorail station and the lake is utilized to display a selection of *Dendrobium* sp orchids, all in the pink, mauve and white shades so popular in Singapore.

↗ Bird shows are held several times a day in an outdoor amphitheatre.

↗ Flamingos have a garden of their own near the entrance to the Park.

→ The smaller of the park's two walk-in aviaries, devoted to southeast Asian birds.

Jurong Bird Park

Started in 1970 in the western industrialized part of Singapore, the Jurong Bird Park has become one of the city's foremost attractions. On display are representatives of more than 350 different species, including the world's largest collection of southeast Asian birds as well as a thriving penguin population. The most celebrated feature is the gigantic walk-in Waterfall Aviary, a man-made valley that contains thousands of plants, a 30.5-m waterfall, and some 1,500 free-flying birds. Another aviary is devoted to regional birds, while a Nocturnal House offers a chance to see various species that are active only at night.

The horticultural side of the Bird Park is equally impressive. Ornamental plants from all over the tropical world have been assembled to create a varied landscape, with particular emphasis on Heliconias, gingers and related species. In 1998, the Heliconia Society International selected Jurong as the site for a major conference that brought together several hundred lovers of this exotic plant.

← Mist drifts along a stream in the lofty Waterfall Aviary, creating the effect of a tropical rain forest.

→ A man-made waterfall cascades more than 30 metres through the jungle-like planting.

The National Parks

In 1967, less than two years after Singapore became a fully independent republic and in the midst of dealing with grave social and economic problems, Prime Minister Lee Kuan Yew launched the Garden City concept. His reasoning was simple. As he expressed it in a speech as Senior Minister at the opening of the National Orchid Garden in 1995, he believed that "a blighted urban jungle of concrete destroys the human spirit" and that the greenery of nature was needed "to lift up our spirits".

The results have been spectacular by any standards. From 700 hectares of parkland in 1967, the total area, excluding nature reserves, has risen to nearly 4000, or 0.67 for every 1,000 people. In 1998, Singapore had 42 regional parks and 210 neighborhood parks scattered throughout the island, not to mention numerous imaginative roadside gardens, shady trees along most roads, and some 33.7 km of "park connectors", which provide a link between parks for joggers and cyclists. The Prime Minister himself played an active role in these efforts; it was he, for instance, who suggested the use of the creeping fig vine (*Ficus pumila*) to disguise overpasses and other bits of exposed cement.

Singapore's parks serve a variety of purposes. Nearly all are recreational, providing facilities to relieve the stress of city life. Many have playgrounds for children and restaurants and cafés. Some offer a history lesson, like Fort Canning Park, where Raffles built his first house, or Labrador Park, a semi-wild oasis around massive fortifications built by the British for the island's defence before World War II. Others have wild areas for bird watching and other nature studies. And some plantings can be seen as proud statements, like the famous highway leading into the city from Changi Airport (see pages 156°160). A blaze of colorful Cannas, Bougainvillea, and other ornamentals, it introduces the Garden City to newcomers in the most dramatic way possible.

← Various palms, red Cordylines, and ever-blooming *Heliconia psittacorum* in the Toa Payoh Park.

↑ The East Coast Park situated on reclaimed land stretching from the downtown area to Changi airport is a popular recreational centre. Cycling and jogging tracks, food and music venues, and the ever-popular beach are the main attractions.

↑ *Monstera deliciosa*, popularly known as the Swiss Cheese Plant, grows easily in Singapore's climate. It is here planted in Bukit Batok Nature Park.

↗ Lining the road leading to Telok Blangah Hill Park is a row of yellow-flowering *Xanthostemon chrysanthus* trees. Introduced from Australia through the Botanic Gardens, they are now widely used in public plantings.

→ Walkways designed by Richard Tan, one of the republic's renowned landscape architects, lead down to the sea in Labrador Park. The park was once the site of a battery of massive guns intended to protect Singapore from attack.

All these parks and plantings come under the management of the National Parks Board, which maintains and regularly upgrades the older parks, plans new ones, and works with both private developers and government agencies in selecting trees and shrubs for various projects. In 1998, it was responsible for nearly a million trees and eight million shrubs. It also maintains a huge nursery to ensure a regular supply of healthy plant material (see pages 112–113) and sponsors such programs as exhibitions to encourage high-rise apartment gardening and the Adopt-a-Park Scheme, under which schools and other organizations (including the Singapore Police Force) have "adopted" various parks and nature areas and reserves. The result has been the transformation of Singapore into a lush garden city in only three decades.

↖ Dwarf coconut palms have been planted along a stretch of beach at Changi. At their base is an underplanting of *Ipomoea pes-caprae*, a beach ground cover. In the distance is Pulau Ubin, a small island off the northeast coast of Singapore.

← Situated at the top northernmost point of the island, Sembawang Park is a small intimate park overlooking the Straits of Johore. A venerable Rain tree is on right.

Airport Road

Roads leading to and from the airports that serve most of the world's capitals are notable for their drabness, passing as they usually do through some of the city's least desirable real estate. Singapore is an exception. On leaving Changi International Airport, newcomers encounter a singular example of the city's green policy in the form of what looks like a vast, luxuriant garden through which an expressway happens to run. Huge, decorative trees – Angsanas, Rain trees, Yellow and Red Flame trees, Mahogany, and various fruit trees among them – rise along both sides above beds planted with masses of colourful shrubs and sweeping, neatly-trimmed lawns. Overhead walkways are softened by creeping fig vine and cascading Bougainvillea that seems perpetually in bloom, while highway dividers are equally lush and varied. Planted with Cannas, Heleconias, and other flowering shurbs, they make for a colourful welcome to Singapore.

← ← The main highway leading up to the airport and its town is lined with Bougainvillea and golden *Duranta repens*. Even the lamposts are covered with Bougainvillea.

↑ A row of Traveller's Palms (*Ravenala madagascariensis*) greets the newcomer to Singapore.

← An avenue of *Terminalia catappa* or Sea Almond trees on a road leading away from the airport adjacent to the sea. Easily recognized by their candelabra form, they have radiating branches that grow at regular intervals from the trunk.

← ← The Bamboo Garden in Terminal 1, rising below a glass-roof atrium area. Species include the Buddha Belly Bamboo (*Bambusa ventricosa*), the Golden Bamboo (*Schizostachynum zollingeri*) and the low-growing Fern Leaf Bamboo (*Bambusa multiplex* "fern leaf"). The Bamboo orchid *Arundiaa graminfolia* (an indigenous orchid) is on left in the foreground.
← Palms, ferns, and orchids along a koi pond in Terminal 2. Among the specimens are the Chinese Fan palm, the Ruffle Fan palm, and the West Indian fern tree.
↓ A constantly renewed and replaced display of flowering orchid plants are placed among the foliage plants that are more tolerant of artificial light.

Changi Airport

Changi Airport, Singapore's Gateway, has been chosen the world's best airport facility in countless international polls. Principally, of course, this is due to the smooth efficiency with which passengers move through its two terminals; but a significant part of Changi's appeal lies in its changing series of horticultural displays. These are developed and maintained by the Civil Aviation Authority of Singapore, with assistance from the National Parks Board, and range from flowers to full-sized plants. One stand, for instance, highlights Singapore's famous orchids, especially a sampling of hybrids named after statesmen and dignitaries. Another brings together a collection of rare palms and ferns around a pond of brightly-coloured koi. There is also a display of various Bamboos, dramatically lit by a skylight, a rooftop Cactus garden complete with rocks and stones, and numerous planter boxes with Philodendrons and cascading orchid sprays.

← Planes take off and land next to the Cactus Garden, which displays such specimens as the Prickly Pear, the Column Cactus, and the Golden Barrel (*Echinocactus grusonii*).

↙ Assorted Cacti thrive in a rooftop garden on Terminal 1. All the specimens are labelled along the pathways that lead through the dry, rocky landscape. The white leaves in the lower picture are an Agave, while the tall plants in the background are the so-called Dragon Tree (*Dracaena draco*).

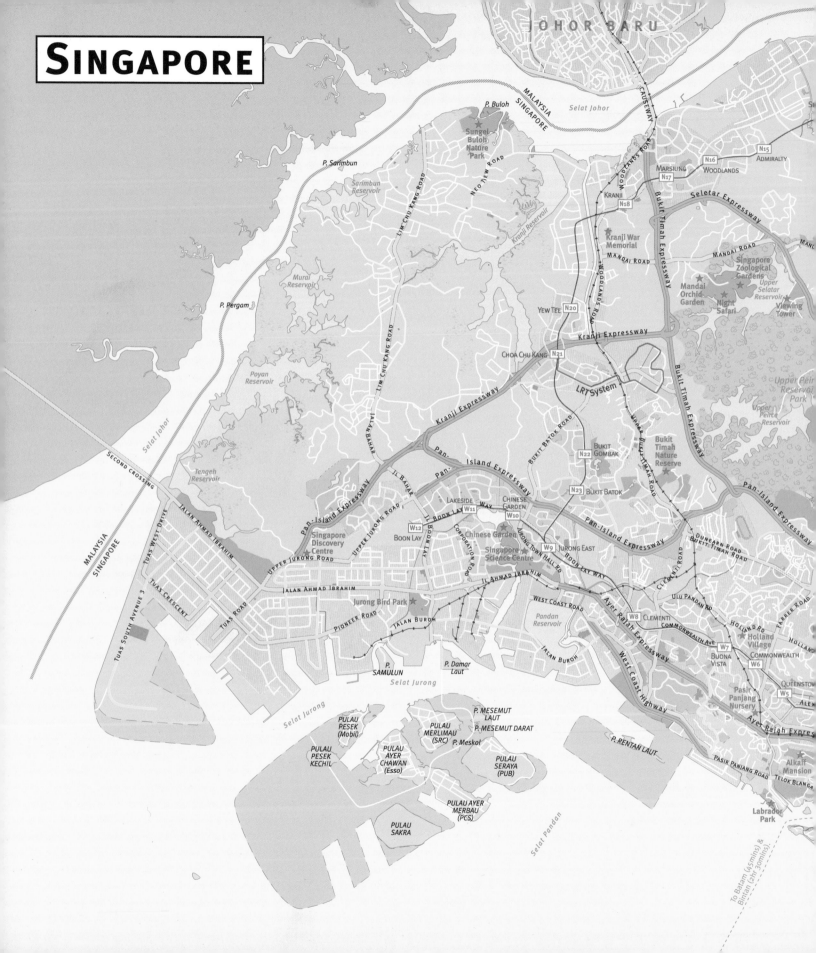